Stranger Than Fiction

A Criminal Defense Attorney's Memoir, New York, New York

by

Richard Siracusa, Esq.

DORRANCE
PUBLISHING CO
EST. 1920
PITTSBURGH, PENNSYLVANIA 15238

Dorrance Publishing Co
585 Alpha Drive
Pittsburgh, PA 15238
Visit our website at *www.dorrancebookstore.com*

ISBN: 978-1-4809-5449-6
eISBN: 978-1-4809-5402-1

IN MEMORIAM: JOSEPH JACK BERNARD, ESQ.

(1944-2016)

TABLE OF CONTENTS

Chapter 1 Beginnings 1

Chapter 2 Paralegally Speaking 9

Chapter 3 Crazy Love 15

Chapter 4 Dance With Me, Etta 19

Chapter 5 Falling In Love With Love Or Love's Labour's Lost 27

Chapter 6   His Vision Of Reality Was Not At All Like Ours:

    The Midtown Slasher 39

Chapter 7 The Madness Of Two 61

Chapter 8 The Troll And The Five Hundred Pound Woman 73

Chapter 9 The Night The Music Died 89

Chapter 10 The Vietnamese Kinnaree: Illusion And Disillusion 109

Chapter 11 Driving South In the Northbound Lane 119

Chapter 12 Tones For Jones Bones Or You're Never Too Old For Love .127

Chapter 13 Fields Of Ambrosia 133

Chapter 14 Mohamed Said: "Show Me The Money" 143

1. Beginnings

When I was in college as an undergraduate, it was the early 1960s, Russia had already put a cosmonaut in orbit and the United States was playing catch up. JFK had promised to put a man on the moon by the end of the decade, the government was screaming for scientists and engineers and the radio blasted the strains of "Sput-nick-Sput-nick sputa-nicka-chick."." Every student wanted to be a scientist or engineer with visions of working for NASA to help fulfill the prophecy their recently fallen leader. Besides you could make a whopping $10,000 to $15,000 per year if you were lucky. It was definitely not the time to be writing your PhD dissertation on the influence of Chaucer upon modern American literature. I had no such aspirations because I was, at best, a mediocre student with absolutely no aptitude for mathematics or engineering. I knew that whatever talents I might have would certainly not fit very well into the work-a-day world as it then existed. I knew what I was and I also knew that no one outside of my immediate family would want to pay me a livable wage given my academic credentials. It was also a time when the Viet Nam war debacle was just ramping up. JFK had been struck down and Lyndon B. Johnson was our president. Johnson promised both "guns and butter" as he prosecuted the savage war in Viet Nam which cost nearly 60,000 American lives and countless wounded and maimed all for no good reason. As the war built to a crescendo, Johnson pumped as much money into the economy as he did into the war only this was his "war on poverty." There were jobs galore a few years after I had graduated from college but when I actually did graduate, I could only get a job as an insurance salesman or a school teacher at a thrilling $4,500 per year and even those professions were skeptical of my academic credentials. My father was a very good insurance salesman without a high school education and I did not want to be like him. Don't get me wrong, I loved my father but I thought why did I waste four years in college to achieve the same plateau as my dad who did not have even a high school diploma? So I made the first of what would be many foolish missteps generally attributed to many young men of my age with little or no good judgment. I joined the Marine Corps.

I joined the Corps upon the advice of my college roommate who made a career of the Marine Corps and retired as a two-star General. We had opposite personalities and different ambitions or rather he fulfilled his greatest ambition while I remained confused for several years after I received my degree. He did two glorious tours in Viet Nam and I ended up in a Naval Hospital near Camp LaJeune, North Carolina fighting for my young, useless life after developing such a severe case of viral pneumonia that I received the last rites of the Catholic Church. I don't think the last rites would have made much difference when I reached the pearly gates, but they gave them to me anyway. At a time when Lyndon Johnson was sending every "swinging dick" to Viet Nam, as my old drill instructor would euphemistically put it, the Marine Corps wanted to get me well enough to become fodder for an infantry platoon fighting off the Viet Cong in some rain soaked mud hole in the Mekong Delta. I had other ideas. If I had survived my near fatal mistake in joining the Marine Corps, I was getting the hell out of the Marines as quickly as possible.

I was so ill and it was taking so long for my lungs to clear that the Marines offered me a choice. I could continue in the Corps on limited duty until I got well enough to get shot in Viet Nam or they would put me on extended leave status and send me home with the possibility that if the tender, loving care of my mother did not get me well enough to continue, there was the probability that I would be honorably discharged before my time. Are you fucking kidding me? I quickly bribed a fellow patient in the hospital to give his own blood sample in placed of mine because I still had too many white blood corpuscles per cubic milliliter than him. My body was still fighting off the infection even after nearly two months in the hospital and the medics would not release me until my white blood cell count went below a certain number. His white blood cell count had reached that level. Finally, I was on the verge of getting out of that shithole hospital with palmetto bugs so big I could have hopped on the back of one of them and flown back to my parent's home in upstate New York. I packed my bags and took my painfully calloused ass from too many penicillin shots out through the front gate shoving most of my Marine Corps equipment into a nearby barrel and I kissed the United States Marine Corps goodbye forever.

After spending a few months with my parents recuperating, they grew weary of my constant late hour sojourns into the taverns of my hometown with my high school friends. My recuperation process had taken on a certain unacceptable quality of life suitable to my parents tastes and they insisted on the unthinkable. They wanted me to get a job. So I submitted my applications to Eastman Kodak and Xerox who were the large corporate employers located in the Rochester area. I had lost a lot of weight when I was in the hospital largely due to the uneatable food they served in the hospital of no return and, of course, my illness. I presented myself for the employment interviews looking like a patient who had just been released from a psychiatric hospital. Thin, sickly pallor, bulging eyes complete with a suit that looked as if it was provided by Goodwill. You could reasonably infer as we say in the legal profession, my presence was not exactly commanding. The interviewers quickly calculated the cost of medical insurance premiums if they were to hire me and just as quickly, I was shown the door. It was after several forays into the land of opportunity as I have just described that I decided to take by now healed ass from the comforting care of my parents and move to the only place on earth where I would not stand out-New York City. Thus began the great adventure that would consume most of the rest of my life and form the basis of this narrative.

One hot day in the summer of 1967, I packed my meager belongings, borrowed money from my life insurance policy and hopped a Greyhound Bus for the big city just as Ratso Rizzo would do a few years later in Midnight Cowboy only Ratso was leaving New York.

My first job in New York was at the famous men's clothier, Brooks Brothers located on Madison Avenue. When I started that job I was living in a furnished room with a kitchen alcove in Jackson Heights in the borough of Queens. I had taken up residence there upon the advice of a Greyhound bus driver who assured me that Jackson Heights was full of gorgeous airline stewardesses who were hot for a good time. They chose Jackson Heights because of its proximity to LaGuardia airport. Needless to say after a couple of months in the Heights, I never met any stewardesses, hot or otherwise, so I took the advice of a colleague who worked at Brooks brothers and moved to a now extinct hotel called the Winslow which was located at 55th and Madison just ten short blocks from Brooks Bros. But before I left the confines of my apartment in Queens, I made a fateful decision. I took the Law School Aptitude Test. I studied very hard for it and much to my surprise, I did extremely well. I knew that the L.S.A.T had a four-year window in which I could apply to law school.

I didn't exactly think of being a lawyer at any time in my life but I knew that I did not want to be a salesman and end up like Willie Loman or a glorified stock boy as I was at Brooks Bros. My residence at the Winslow and my job at Brooks Bros. afforded me the unparalleled opportunity to indulge in my greatest passion, lounging in the great jazz clubs of New York, listening to the masters produce some of the greatest music of its time. Clubs like the original Birdland, the Metropole Café, the Five Spot and the Hickory House were still in existence. You could walk into those places, pay a few dollars cover, buy one drink and listen for the entire evening. No one bothered you a so long as you behaved. I became a New York Rangers fan listening to the great Marv Albert on the radio announcing the drama of a "kick save and a beauty." This was, of course, decades before we learned of Marv's predilection for cross dressing and biting.

My internship at Brooks Bros. lasted only six months. I was making less than $5,000 per year and the only money I ever had was in my pocket. Besides, I was getting tired of trying to climb either the corporate ladder or the ladder which led me to the very heights of the stockroom which I was obliged to navigate to retrieve or re-stock the inventory. My parents were becoming skeptical of my explanations as to why I had no meaningful job and no prospects for a meaningful life for more than three years after I had received my B.S. Some of those included: "stop giving me a hard time," "I'm still feeling the effects of the pneumonia," "I nearly died," and "if I can make it in New York, I can make it anywhere," anticipating the famous phrase before Frank Sinatra had a chance to record it. It was at this time that I shelved my corporate ambitions with Brooks Bros. and applied for employment with the U.S. Public Health Service but not before I managed to liberate an expensive suit especially made for someone else who was my exact size. With that suit in tow, I started the job as an epidemiologist tracking down the sexual contacts of those unfortunates afflicted with venereal disease.

In the late 60s, AIDS had not yet been identified so most of what we dealt with were cases of either gonorrhea or syphilis also called "the French disease." I always thought it quaint that the French known for their legendary love making would have a disease of equally legendary destruction named after them. It was an employ which would hold me in good stead for what I was to experience in my career as a criminal defense attorney. My colleagues and I worked the entire borough of Manhattan but we mainly concentrated our efforts on the upper west side. It is very trendy now but back then the west side was honeycombed with single room occupancy hotels which were regularly populated by drug addicts, convicted felons, prostitutes and ambulatory paranoid schizophrenics. Half way houses abounded as did the houses of assignation along West End Avenue that posed as buildings in which you would have no objection to having your college aged daughter rent an apartment. West 80th Street, particularly between Central Park West and Columbus Avenue, was so dangerous that we used to joke that the police would have to close it every few hours to carry out the dead bodies. Now the entire area is so gentrified you could hardly imagine what went on nearly fifty years ago. Zabars has taken over the whole block at the expense of an SRO called the Broadway Central which occupied the upper floors of the building for decades before Eli Zabar managed to close it and turn it into the appliance and houseware section of his famous store.

We dealt mainly with young gay men ranging in age from emancipated minors to those in their late forties. I did break the mold one time when a prostitute named Carol Matthews walked into our clinic on West 100th St. exhibiting the symptoms of primary syphilis. Not to worry about poor Carol. The disease is easily treatable with penicillin at that stage with little or no permanent damage to the body. It is when the disease is allowed to fester in the body for several years that the permanent damage is done. In its tertiary stage, the disease acts like a cancer, eating away at any organ it chooses to invade including the brain. Tertiary syphilis will cause permanent brain damage and eventually death.

I was assigned the task of interviewing Carol Matthews for her sexual contacts. She seemed to like my schoolboy charm which consisted mainly of staring at her breasts and legs as she handed over her little black book with the names of over 300 of her regular customers. Most of them were Chinese men living in Chinatown (where else?) We sent for reinforcements from the other clinics around Manhattan and we spread out on the lower east side. The contents of Matthew's little black book led to the treatment of an untold number of those infected as the cases of syphilis fell from the sky like the loaves and fishes. It fed our clinical work product for many months afterward. From that time forward, I was known as the "hooker specialist" and given the task of interviewing every prostitute who walked into the clinic. Most of them were surly drug addicts with understandably bad attitudes toward men. I was lucky with Carol Matthews.

It was a record for epidemiological investigation at that time and made me a star. But my star shone brightly for only a very short time then burned itself out when, at the end of my employment probationary period, I was refused permanent status and summarily dismissed. My original supervisor had been promoted and the new one did not like my cavalier attitude toward punctuality. Why should you work eight hours per day when you could get the work done in five or six? After all, I was in the field most of the day. So my new supervisor handed me my gold starred certificate of merit and hustled me out the front door but not before I embarrassed him by not resigning as agreed thereby forcing him to fire me. During the last two weeks of my employment, I ignored all his orders, avoided all the meetings and generally was a total pain in the ass until my final day when I told him that he was an incompetent leader who suffered from problems of sexual inadequacy. My decision not to resign allowed me to collect unemployment insurance which was my main objective.

Like my near fatal bout of pneumonia which allowed me to escape the Marine Corps before my time, my experience as an epidemiologist for only one year and my eventual dismissal was another blessing in disguise. It had introduced me to an alternate life style. One that I could never have imagined. That experience would become an invaluable asset for life as a defense attorney. During that short time with the U.S. Health Service, I got a rare glimpse into the underbelly of society and the misfits which formed its population. I saw drug addiction and mental illness on a first-hand basis. I witnessed the death of a young prostitute who bled to death after attempting to self–abort her unwanted fetus. The death of a resident of a seedy SRO hotel who staggered out the door of the hotel holding his chest which had a large hole blown into it by a shotgun. My colleagues and I witnessed drug overdoses on a weekly basis. On one occasion, we saw a limousine with shades covering the windows parked in a section of Harlem not usually frequented by limousines. I was told by a police officer no less that it was probably Judy Garland in the limo trying to score drugs. I can't say if the cop was right, but she did die of a drug overdose about a year later. Most importantly, it was an experience which allowed me to answer my mother's timeless question: "Richard, how do homosexuals get syphilis?" An answer I could have never provided prior to my short life as an epidemiologist.

II. Paralegally Speaking

After I was cured of my venereal disease employment at the Public Health Service, I did what many of the recent college graduates of that time did. I took advantage of the money the Johnson administration had poured into poverty programs in New York and became a social worker with the New York City Department of Social Services. Yes, what they say about social work was generally true. The system destroyed the lives of the recipients of public assistance and burnt out the dedicated workers trying to make a difference leaving only those workers who simply did not give a shit. In order to survive on a one-to-one basis with our clients, the workers who really did give a shit would look for a way around the stupid rules of engagement by simply ignoring the rules or breaking the law. The system was just throwing money at the recipients instead of trying to find a solution to the endless cycle of poverty begetting welfare begetting still more poverty. My favorite devise to skirt the rules was to have my unit and case supervisor sign the authorizations which provided money for the recipients who were moving within the five boroughs of New York City. I would change the amount on the authorizations using a method the secret of which will go with me to my grave. My clients would then have enough money to move to another state and hopefully to another life. Anything to get them out of the ghettos of Harlem or the worst place in the world, the South Bronx. You'll remember the pictures taken of the Bronx during the 1977 World Series by the blimp flying over Yankee stadium showing the horrifying picture of the burning building not far from the Stadium. That was the South Bronx in the good old days compared to what we encountered as caseworkers in 1968.

When I was assigned to a social services center in the South Bronx, we would make field visits in packs of four to six caseworkers, leave our wallets and valuables locked up at the center and put a few dollars and subway tokens in our shoes. The streets were a war zone and we were its fodder. Heroin was a plague and the addicts would try to pry the fillings out of your teeth or worse if you did not try to avoid them. On one occasion, I had to go to Kelly St. in the south Bronx to visit a client who was dying of cancer and receiving little or no care out of indifference or fear. Woe to those who enter this portal alone which is exactly what I had to do trying to pass myself off as a junkie looking to score drugs. Kelly St. was one of the most dangerous places in the Bronx, if not the entire city. I wore a thin autumn windbreaker in February, my hair was uncombed and I was unshaven. My sneakers had holes in them but I did have some money and subway tokens in a bag stuffed into my crotch. When I hit Kelly Street, I thought I had thought of everything to camouflage myself except the most important thing. I was the only white guy for miles around. The denizens of Kelly street knew exactly who I was but took sympathy on me because they also knew that I was there to help the sick lady in the building down the street.

The only real advantage to the job was the fact that if you were breathing and had a heartbeat, you fulfilled all the necessary requirements to be a social worker. Those were also the exact requirements that would get you convicted of a RICO crime in the federal courts as I later learned. Myself and many of my co-workers took full advantage of that standard by simply walking away from our jobs to spend the summer or longer periods in Europe and then returning without so much as a by your leave. I took off for months traveling to every country in Europe and staying with my cousins in Italy. The Department of Social Services was happy to have me back when I finally returned. But I was assigned to the south Bronx in the area I have previously described as a punishment for my unauthorized vacation. By this time my parents had completely given up on me but I did feel their pain and in 1969 I decided to apply to law school.

My scores on the L.S.A.T. were getting stale. I had sown my wild oats and I had traveled extensively which is what I really wanted to do before I got serious about life. It took me a few years to accomplish my objective but I did exactly what I wanted to do and I had a great time doing it. I was satisfied and now it was time to deal with my future. The immediate future included continuing my tenure at the Department of Social Services and the study of law at the New York Law School, evening division starting in the fall of 1969. I celebrated my acceptance to law school by (you guessed it) taking another unauthorized absence from the entreaties of my long-suffering case supervisor at the welfare center.

I took off the summer months on the west coast in San Francisco and its environs. At that time I was living on East 7th St. just across the way from Tompkins Square Park which was the epicenter of hippies, phony Buddhist monks spreading venereal disease, mind expanding drugs, flower children and free love. The monks were particularly obnoxious. I interviewed many of them when they would come to the health clinic when I was with the public health service. They would arrive with filthy robes that stunk of urine and semen, dirt encrusted bodies particularly on their shaven heads, with genitals in hand bent over in pain. Gonorrhea was their specialty disease which spread like wildfire among the many faithful seeking nirvana.

When I got to San Francisco that summer, I discovered a similar situation in the Haight-Ashbury. Both scenes had disintegrated into rampant drug use, alcoholism and crime with little inclination towards changing the system. A similar situation happened forty years later with the Occupy Wall St. movement. In reality, both movements lasted less than a year. I ran around the San Francisco area for several weeks living with friends, sleeping on the beach at Monterrey, smoking grass and generally enjoying my last period of total irresponsibility before sinking into the abyss of law school study. The evening division is a part time program which, at that time, took four years to complete instead of the usual three years. I had to work to put myself through school and during my first year I remained with the Department of Social Services who were foolish enough to rehire me after my second unauthorized vacation in as many years. I really felt bad about seeming to waste my parent's hard-earned money which had provided me with my undergraduate education. I took no money from them even after I had revealed to them that I had successfully completed my first year of law school. I had stopped eating the hash brownies baked by my late friend Harvey Herzog and had imposed a Spartan like regiment of study upon myself which would permit me to successfully complete the heavy burden of law school. Harvey was a native New Yorker who was a voracious reader who convinced me I could make it through law school and was my best friend in New York in the early years. He died suddenly in 2011. I really wanted to learn about the criminal justice system, so in the fall of 1970, I walked into the office of Milton Adler the attorney-in-chief of the Legal Aid Society and offered my services as a paralegal.

Adler was a brilliant attorney who had been a public defender since the late 1940s twenty years before the Supreme Court of the United States ruled that indigents were constitutionally entitled to an attorney and Legal Aid was considered either a new soft drink or a reference manual for non-lawyers. Milton was the best. An uncommon individual who had dedicated his life to the poor and for very little pay. He was a brusque individual which hid a very big heart. He looked at me skeptically and proceeded to scold me when I laughed inappropriately at one of his remarks mistaking it for a joke. The interview was not going well when suddenly I saw his eyes brighten as if an idea had just come into his head. He told me that even though I had virtually no experience, there was an attorney who had worked for the Legal Aid Society for many years who specialized in post-conviction remedies and he had a need for a legal assistant. It would a perfect marriage between attorneys who had loads of experience with a fledgling law student with absolutely none.

Post-conviction remedies include writs of habeas corpus and motions to reduce the sentence for those who had already been convicted. Habeas corpus is a remedy challenging the detention of those who are illegally incarcerated and has its roots in English common law going back to the Middle Ages. The attorney to whom I was assigned was an untrustworthy individual with a corrosive personality who would belittle you for no good reason other than to satisfy his profound sense of insecurity. But he was brilliant with a thorough knowledge of habeas corpus which was his specialty. He wielded the habeas corpus writ like a sword and accomplished the release of several individuals by sheer force of will.

Working for him was an impossible task and while I learned a lot from him, his destructive personality made my life miserable. I soon learned that he was not to be trusted and would criticize me for the slightest faux pas. I was hired to be his assistant because he had gone through several other assistants all of whom were young attorneys who usually lasted only a few weeks. In those days, you would call him a "screamer." Nowadays, he would be categorized as a "miserable prick." I knew that working as his assistant would probably cause me permanent emotional damage but I needed a job and I really wanted to learn about the criminal justice system. I quickly realized that working for him would be beyond difficult, but it was a unique opportunity rarely afforded any young student of the law.

Rikers Island is the main detention complex in New York City located in the East River. Rikers is a place where both inmates and corrections officers are brutalized. But forty years ago, it was, believe it or not, a safer place where we would be allowed to walk from one facility to another through underground passages which honeycombed the island. No special permits were necessary. No less an entity than the New York Jets would occasionally practice on the regulation sized football field which occupied the center of the island complete with goal posts and bleachers. Inmates would be allowed to view the practice sessions from the few bleachers that were there. Given the situation at Rikers now, it is incredible that anyone not charged with crime or not an employee would voluntarily choose to venture on to Rikers much less than a professional football team. But that was the case in the early 1970s.

We would walk among the inmates and corrections officers as one would walk on a public street. Our main focus was to listen to the complaints of the inmates. Most of the complaints had to do with living conditions and the brutality of the corrections officers. Rikers was run like a gulag but it might be considered a resort in the 70s compared to what it is today. Hopelessly few inmates had real legal problems but we did manage to make inroads into changing the rules which affected them. As a result of our efforts, gay inmates were separated from the general population and inmates who were being held for violations of their parole were assigned attorneys to represent them at their hearings.

Most of the inmates had psychological problems. Some had serious psychological problems. If you weren't crazy before you entered Rikers, the conditions would drive you crazy very quickly. Rapes and assaults were rampant. If you did not learn to defend yourself, you would be victimized by both inmates and officers. The constant roar of the planes taking off and landing at LaGuardia airport, which occurred about every minute or so, were loud enough to blow out your eardrums or cause a concussion. LaGuardia was so close that you could swim to one of its runways. On many occasions, I could not hear the inmate sitting directly across the table from me. The corrections officers would herd the inmates whose already serious mental problems, exacerbated by the previously described inhuman conditions, into the room where we would conduct our interviews. My mentor, who was as unstable as most of our interviewees, would have me do triage for the ones with legal problems while I handled the majority who were as unstable as him. If one of the majority slipped through to his area, there would be weeping and the gnashing of teeth and it would usually require the presence of an officer to subdue the turmoil.

Learning to deal with my mentor was a great experience in learning to deal with the myriad of mental illnesses I encountered at Rikers Island. The corrections officers had no idea of how to handle these inmates except through brute force. When we would show up at Rikers it was a golden opportunity for the officers to dump their problems on to us, or rather on to me. They would leave the disturbed inmates outside the room waiting their turn while telling them that we were the ones who could really help them and then disappear. The paranoid schizophrenics were particularly frightening. The instant they would enter the room you could tell that something was seriously amiss. They would sit in front of you, body frozen in position with eyes wide open in an unblinking stare. The story would usually begin with a recitation of their most recent hospitalizations in the psychiatric ward and what psychotropic medications they were refusing to take because they were not really crazy. When I countered by informing them that I was a "lawyer not a psychiatrist," the stare would become an intense glare. You could tell that they did not want to hear any of my excuses and were thinking of doing me great bodily harm such as stuffing my body sideways into a wood chipper. It was usually a very frightening experience for me as I attempted to change the subject usually without success. On those occasions when I felt that the intense glares might result in violence, I would stand up slowly, grab the small of my back and grimace in pain attempting to convince the agitated inmate in front of me that I was already in pain and that he need not inflict more. This maneuver usually distracted the inmate long enough for me to bolt out the door of the interview room. Fortunately, this did not happen very often but often enough that I would position my chair closer to the door each time it did happen. This phase of my legal life led to my first brush with celebrity.

III. Crazy Love

Thursdays was writ day in the Bronx Supreme Court when we would argue the Writs of Habeas Corpus on behalf of the inmates. When we came across an interesting legal issue, we would submit a more formal writ but most of the writs were submitted by the inmates themselves. Those types of writs were called pro se writs, or do it yourself writs. Most of them had to do with administrative issues such as incorrect jail time calculations, outstanding warrants that needed to be cleared up or the lack of medical care. The inmates were smart enough but as you might expect, they were poorly educated. It would take some effort to read their pro se writs to get at what they were trying to say. It would take me three or four hours to wade through the writs so we would be able to make semi-intelligent arguments to the judge. It put me in mind of an inmate named Gideon in Florida who was convicted and sentenced to a lengthy term of imprisonment in the early 1960s without benefit of an attorney. Gideon could not afford an attorney and Florida did not provide one. Gideon sent a handwritten letter to the United States Supreme Court full of grammatical errors and misspellings led by the late Chief Justice Earl Warren. That letter led to the landmark case of Gideon v. Wainwright which reversed the conviction and mandated that the state had to provide an attorney to all those defendants who could not afford one. Gideon changed the entire manner in which criminal cases were prosecuted in the United States. Nothing quite so earth shattering, but we did manage to right a few lesser wrongs perpetrated by the criminal justice system in New York City.

On those Thursdays when we were in the Bronx Supreme Court arguing the writs, I would sometimes notice a short, middle-aged man wearing glasses and goatee and always dressed in the same suit. The suit was neatly pressed but you could tell that it had seen better days. This man would go from courtroom to courtroom shaking hands with all the judges. He looked and dressed like a lawyer but he carried no briefcase and make no formal appearances on the record in any of the courtrooms he entered. I asked my mentor if he knew this man. He told me that his name was Burt Pugach and that he had been convicted of hiring a hit man to throw lye in the face of his much younger mistress who was attempting to end their relationship. Pugach had been a successful lawyer dealing with mostly personal injury cases in the Bronx and flew his own plane before his conviction and ultimate disbarment. The judges in the Bronx were his friends and they continued to treat him as such even after he was convicted. Some even sent him gifts mostly in the form of clothing while he was incarcerated. It was obvious that none of the judges had ever sent him a new suit. I asked my mentor how he knew this man. He responded as to the circumstances of his incarceration and long sentence. I inquired as to when he had finished his long sentence and was told that Pugach was still serving his sentence but the Department of Corrections allowed him to wander the halls of justice in the Bronx untethered every Thursday for the entire day when the writs were argued. When it was time to return to his state digs located at maximum security prison not far from New York City, he would merely return to the back of the courthouse and be whisked away by his awaiting chariot in the form of a Department of Corrections bus. This was more than forty years ago. I can only imagine what the media would do with this story if it happened today.

Burt was a very successful attorney who was making a ton of money from his personal injury practice when met a young raven-haired beauty in a Bronx park named Linda Riis. Pugach was instantly smitten with Linda. She had jet black hair and her eyes were so strikingly dark that they seemed to be two deep pools set in the middle of her face. Pugach was several years older than Riis and had been married for many years. Neither circumstance seemed to deter Pugach from the pursuit of his quarry. It seemed to awaken his dormant libido and a romantic relationship was soon formed. The relationship continued for a couple of years but it was the old story of a much older married man and the naïve younger woman. She demanded marriage. He promised divorce but neither happened. Riis took up with a man of her own generation while Pugach spun completely out of control. He neglected his practice and when her engagement to the much younger man was announced, he self-destructed. No younger man was going to have Linda and if he couldn't drown himself in those dark pools, then he would drain those pools of their vitality forever.

Pugach hired a convicted felon to ambush Linda near her home to throw lye in her face. The lye accomplished its objective by not only scarring her beautiful face but destroying the usefulness of those incredibly beautiful eyes. She had some vision for several years after the attack, but gradually lost all her vision by the time she reached middle age. Neither Pugach nor his hired gun were master criminals and were captured and charged very soon after the attack. Both received long prison sentences. I encountered Pugach as he was nearing the end of his sentence but he still had a few years left before he was eligible for parole. This might explain the somewhat laissez-faire attitude of the New York State Department of Corrections towards Pugach when he was brought to the Bronx on Thursdays in the early 1970s. He was a brilliant attorney who used his brains to make enough money to buy and fly his own plane but threw his life away on a beautiful woman. Pugach had sold his soul to the devil for youth and the love of the much younger Linda Riis just as Faust had sold his soul for youth and the love of the beautiful Marguerite. I would meet Pugach nearly every Thursday in the Bronx Supreme Court. He recognized my mentor and began referring us to recent cases in our area of expertise. We would nod our heads in recognition or shake hands every time we would meet. He helped us but his primary objective was to assist his fellow inmates in filing their lawsuits. Usually this kind of behavior would label any other inmate as a troublemaker and earn him a sixty-day bit in the "bing," otherwise known as the "box" or in civilian terms: solitary confinement. If that didn't work, then the offending inmate would "ride the bus" or be switched to a different facility and then switched again when this behavior continued at the new facility. Pugach was immune from all of this and he was a great help to us and his fellow inmates all the while snubbing his nose at the machinations of the Department of Corrections.

One time I decided to conduct my own investigation into the rumor of a weekly illicit liaison between Pugach and Linda Riis somewhere in the bowels of the Bronx Supreme Court. I followed him making his rounds in the court for a few hours but I saw no liaison illicit or otherwise. You're probably asking yourself why would Linda have anything to do with Burt after what he done to her? Well the relationship never really ended. While Burt was completing his long prison term, Linda waited for him like Cio-Cio San waited for Pinkerton in Puccini's classic opera "Madame Butterfly" and they were married shortly after Pugach's release. Poor Cio-Cio San suffered a different fate. She committed hara-kiri when Pinkerton showed up several years later with a new wife to claim the son he had fathered with Cio-Cio San. The relationship between Linda and Burt remained tempestuous throughout their marriage until Linda's death in 2013. He might be considered as big a heal as Pinkerton but Linda and Burt's love was as timeless as the sunrise surviving the most trying of circumstances. It was truly a crazy love affair understood only by those afflicted with the same compulsion.

IV. Dance With Me, Etta

My acquaintanceship with Burt Pugach came to a sudden end when I woke up one day and decided that I had had enough of my bipolar mentor. I walked into the office of the attorney in charge of the Legal Aid Society (not Milton Adler) and requested a transfer. That would have been a reasonable request under ordinary circumstances except that the attorney in charge was best friends and a business partner with my tormenter in the Bronx. I had a couple of more years of study left. I was working during the day and going to school at night. In between, I was losing my mind. If I tried to stick it out with my mentor/ tormenter, my studies would have most assuredly suffered. The attorney in charge took pity on me and transferred me to the Manhattan office although I could tell that he did not like double crossing his friend and business partner. I paid for it dearly two years later after I had earned my degree and passed the bar when I applied for a job with the Legal Aid Society as an attorney and was ignored.

After being transferred to Manhattan, I discovered that I had acquired a unique knowledge of the criminal courts system. In the early 1970s, training with the Legal Aid Society consisted mostly of trial by ordeal. The new attorney would be handed a full complement of cases and told to do a good job. The new attorneys, while very bright and dedicated, were befuddled. I, on the other hand, knew the courts like the back of my hand. I was not an attorney but I navigated the courthouse like my old friend, Burt Pugach. As a senior law student, I was permitted to argue bail reduction applications before the justices of the Supreme Court in New York County. When a person is initially arrested, he is brought in front of a lower court judge who would either set bail or release the individual based upon several factors including the severity of the offense and prior criminal record. The Justices of the Supreme Court had the power to change the bail status. One of my very first bail reduction applications involved one of the most famous rhythm and blues singers of her time, Etta James. James's career covered more than five decades and she had super hits like "At Last" and, in the 1950s, "Dance With Me, Henry."

She was a great talent and an outstanding performer who was beset by the twin demons of alcoholism and drug addiction for most of her adult life. On this particular occasion, she had been arrested for buying and possessing heroin in an undercover sting in midtown Manhattan. The bail set by the lower court judge was not exceptionally excessive given her prior criminal record and admitted use of heroin. My job was to gather more information about the circumstances of the arrest and to contact any friend or family member who would be willing to post the bail.

I contacted James's record label but they refused to post the bail. So, I sat down with my fellow music buddy and paralegal, Terry Lasky, who came up with the idea of contacting Esmond Edwards who was the A&R guy for James's record label. Edwards told us that the record company was fed up with James's drug use and her erratic behavior. Etta would consistently come to recording sessions either falling-down drunk or wasted on heroin. They knew that poor Etta spent most of her money on drugs and could not make even minimal bail. The record company refused to post the bail as a means of trying to teach her a lesson, a futile effort to be sure when dealing with a drug addict. They also hoped that whatever time she would spend in jail would dry her out enough for her to function as a performer and recording artist. Also, fallacious reasoning since drugs are readily available to any inmate who had the money. When Terry and I convinced Edwards, the record company and the justice who heard my bail application that it would be in James's best interest not to remain in jail, she was released. Etta was so happy to be released from jail that she invited Terry and me to her next recording session which was only a few days later. So, one bitterly cold night in February we ventured out to the recording studio on the west side. We waited and waited for Etta to appear but as you might expect, she never showed up.

She did exhibit some gratitude for our efforts on her behalf by apologizing for her non-appearance and promising us several of her record albums as a gift. About a week later, she walked into our office with twenty record albums which she carried in her arms from wrist to shoulder like an expert waiter would carry dinners without spilling a crumb. She handed up the record albums to us. I got the right armful and Terry got the left. We were ecstatic to be receiving free record albums from one of the greatest singers of her time. She kissed us both while professing undying gratitude as she handed over the albums. When Etta left and the dust had settled, Terry and I examined our windfall only to discover that out of the total of twenty record album covers that we received exactly two of them contained actual records. The remaining eighteen were devoid of any vinyl. The empty covers were a metaphor for our feelings of emptiness upon our discovery that our expected bounty was merely a cheap trick.

This Chapter was named for Etta James's greatest hit of the 1950s because it was the recording which brought her prominence to a more diverse audience after working the black record circuit for most of her career until that point. James would sing "dance with me, Henry" and a male voice would answer "alright baby." Terry and I danced with Etta and it was, upon reflection, alright with both of us. A great talent should not be vilified for human weaknesses. The Etta James story was ended a few years ago by the new demons of cancer and Alzheimer's. Hopefully she is in a better place dancing with the angels, one of them named Henry.

I cannot conclude this part of my legal career without relating a few more stories of my brief career as a bail application specialist. The justices of the Supreme Court knew that I was a law student working as a paralegal for the Legal Aid Society. On most occasions, I would be assigned from four to six bail applications that were deemed worthy of higher court scrutiny. After my initial appearances in bail review court, the justices knew that I was a law student and not wanting to discourage a student of the law who had not yet had a chance to spread his wings and fly, they would invariably reduce the bail on one or two of the applications. Sometimes it would be very difficult for them to reduce the bail because most of my applications involved defendants who were very well acquainted with the criminal justice system.

On one notable occasion, I appeared in front of the late Honorable Gerald Culkin with a bail application concerning two men with long records who were charged with rape and sodomy. Justice Culkin was a ruddy faced Irishman with a pixie smile and a twinkle in his eye and could easily be mistaken for the mythological leprechaun of the land of his heritage. The complaining witness had a long record of prostitution and petty offenses and a history of drug abuse. Sprinkled among the pages of her extensive criminal history were similar complaints of lost virtue and uninvited anal penetration. The men had long histories of robbery and assault. Justice Culkin who had been on the bench for decades before I arrived pretty much knew what he was dealing with when I made my argument for a bail reduction. This was not the first time he had been called upon to negotiate for a lamppost Lorelei who was dissatisfied with the amount paid to her for services rendered and cried foul. This kind of amorous liaison the criminal defense bar has labeled a "tag team" whereby one male would penetrate using the traditional method while the other would enjoy the more perverse pleasures of bringing up the rear. Upon the conclusion of my argument, Justice Culkin peered over his reading glasses, shot me one of his pixie smiles and asked, "Which one got the dirty end of the stick?" Before I could catch my breath, Justice Culkin announced that he was releasing both men. Later on, the case died a natural death when the complaining witness failed to cooperate with the office of the District Attorney.

Over the course of my long career I have had to make some nonsensical arguments in defense of my client. I have received my share of skeptical glances from jurists who had the misfortune of having to listen to me. But during my law student/bail application phase I made an argument which was so absurd that would make the most outrageously verbose defense attorney wince. I made a bail application for a defendant who had a penchant for separating parking meters from their stanchions in order to gain access to the money contained therein. I told the judge that the prosecutor had misjudged my client's motives. I told him that my client actually drove a compact car which he was able to fit in between two larger cars and was attempting to legitimately park his vehicle in between the larger ones.

"Your honor, my client was actually trying to legally park his car by bringing his own parking meter," I protested.

The judge shot me a look which was reminiscent of the stares of the mentally ill inmates I had dealt with earlier at Rikers Island. He announced that he was of a mind to increase the bail but since I was such a novice he would maintain the status quo. He then summarily dismissed me from his courtroom and proclaimed that he would not let me back in until I had passed the bar and could deal with me on a more professional basis. I knew then that I had hit my stride as a defender of equal justice under the law.

Two other situations stand out in my mind which are worthy of providing a conclusion to this phase of my legal career. One could be titled "The Cowardly Lion" and the other, on a whole different level, "The Defecation Dilemma." I made many bail applications in the courtroom of the late Honorable Donald Massey. Justice Massey was a wonderful man with a big heart. A heart that failed him one day right in front of the courthouse in which he had toiled for so many years. Justice Massey took me under his wing and explained many of the failings of the criminal justice system and the personalities of the judges before whom I would make many of my bail applications.

"If you know the judge, you know what you should say," he instructed me.

I always took his advice and enjoyed being in his courtroom. But there was just one problem. Justice Massey looked just like the actor Bert Lahr who was the cowardly lion in the movie "The Wizard of Oz." He even had Lahr's mannerisms and way of speaking. Each time I would walk into his courtroom, I would envision Justice Massey as Lahr in that ridiculous costume and makeup and start to giggle. After several encounters in his courtroom with my obvious attempts to suppress laughter, one day he saw me sitting in the front row waiting my turn with a smile almost turned to laughter.

He had just finished drinking a cup of water when he turned to one of the court officers and said, "I'll have another" imitating Lahr's inflection and wiggling his nose.

We looked at each other and both laughed heartily. At that point, I knew that he knew. I always looked forward to being in his courtroom. When he died so suddenly, I was heartbroken but resolved that whenever I would be having difficulty with a more demanding judge, I would think of that day when he asked for "another." I wish that there was "Another" like Judge Massey.

In an attempt to significantly reduce length of time to relate the story of the defecation dilemma, I will leave my magazines and newspapers in another room as I enter the toilet to tell my story unencumbered by reading materials. On one nasty day in the winter, a man was being hustled by the police into the arraignment court. The police seemed nervous and I thought that this man had been accused of a particularly heinous crime. I soon discovered that it was not really the heinousness of the crime but what he did to conceal his alleged misbehavior. The man had swallowed (allegedly) a valuable diamond ring which he had managed to pilfer from a very surprised jewelry dealer in the diamond area of Manhattan. The swallower had posed as a dealer by dressing like a night at the opera and exhibiting a rudimentary knowledge of the diamond industry to such an extent that he managed to impress the dealer from here on referred to as the party of the second part or the swallowee. Not to be confusing, but you could reasonably infer with a high degree of certainty that the swallowee had become the swallower of such a remarkable line of bullshit that he handed the expensive ring to our first named swallower/bullshitter who, as you might expect, popped the ring into his mouth and attempted to run out of the store.

The dealer or the party of the second part also known as the swallowee/swallower had other ideas. He tackled the would-be thief before he got to the front door and sat on him while his assistant called the police. When the police arrived, latex glove in hand, they searched the area in which the ring was last seen but no ring was discovered. They then searched the area where our thief had been sat upon with similar results. It was then determined, I assume by a law enforcement higher up, that the ring had, in fact, been swallowed and the only recourse of course, was to let nature take its course. Ergo, the nervousness of the police escorts when the ring swallower was brought to arraignment court. The District Attorney announced to the judge that irrefutably strong evidence as to strength of his case would soon be forthcoming and that the swallower should be held with no bail and confined to single occupancy cell. The judge went one step further and ordered the Department of Corrections to conduct a twenty-four-hour watch of the swallower's activities in the cell and when the critical time was at hand, the Captain of Corrections should immediately be notified. Most importantly, the water valve to the toilet should be placed in the off position so that the evidence would not end up in the vast New York City sewer system with the alligators, snakes and other exotic animals that have been said to reside there.

I got involved with the case when I was notified by the legal aid supervisor that my unusual talents were needed immediately in the Supreme Court before nature had actually taken its course. Of course, I ran up to the Supreme Court and when this particular jurist would see me in his courtroom, he would, on more than one occasion, announce that there was going to be trouble. He was right because in my perceived haste to beat the clock, I uttered one of the seven words forbidden by the FCC on public airways. The word was quickly changed to bowel movement and I struggled on with as much fervor as before the offending word had been uttered. I argued that it was a violation of the swallower's Eighth amendment right against cruel and unusual punishment and a violation of his fourth amendment right as an unwarranted intrusion of his right to privacy to be confined in such a manner. The judge agreed his confinement was cruel and unusual and set a modest bail. The judge had obviously never been in the Marine Corps.

When the judge realized the nature of the bail application, he exhibited a look of calm resignation seemingly to fully know what was about to befall him. When the forbidden word was uttered, he cast his eyes towards the heavens and tucked both of his hands under his chin in an effort to hold the position of his head in place. I don't know if the forbidden word had any real effect on him but he did do the right thing although he probably would have preferred to have been somewhere else when I made the application. I later learned that it took nature more than twenty-four hours to yield the evidence. The swallower was charged with grand larceny and I always wondered whether the ring made it back into the hands of the dealer. I know that in Wagner's four opera Ring Cycle, Brunnhilde threw the cursed ring back into the Rhine from whence it came ending the odyssey of the all-powerful ring which had destroyed the gods. Perhaps the ring which had traversed a human digestive tract was returned to its proper place in the display case as a symbol of the measures law enforcement will take to protect the community.

V. Falling In Love With Love
Or Love's Labours Lost

After nearly four years as a paralegal freely roaming the courthouse like a Bedouin tribesman, the Legal Aid Society decided that I was not Legal Aid material. Mind you, I had worked in the courts for almost four years and knew more about the court system than any of the supervisors for whom I had worked. Those supervisors had been so ill-trained on their way to supervisory status that they were fairly incompetent in performing their duties. They were smart lawyers whose abilities had been corrupted by their lack of proper training at the very beginnings of their careers. As a result, during my tenure as a paralegal, I would go off on my own shunning any attempt at supervision by those in charge. I knew how to get things done because of my experience. They could offer me no better advice that I could offer myself. I did not want to waste time asking questions to which I already knew the answers. If an attorney would come to me with a procedural question, I would attempt to provide an answer sans supervisory input. It was well known to the supervisors that the staff lacked confidence in them and that they would uniformly turn to me as a better alternative. I certainly didn't know the answers to all their questions but I had developed a reputation as the "go to" guy. For this reason, I was resented by all those who had any influence as to the hiring of newly admitted attorneys. This fact, in combination with the BFF relationship between the new attorney-in-charge and my former tormentor, induced me to seek temporary employment as a New York City cabdriver.

There have been a myriad of over educated cabdrivers such as those infamous PhD's in English literature who could find no other alternative, but I had another option. I had a brother in Washington, D.C. who had a convertible couch. So, I took the District of Columbia Bar exam and the New York State Bar exam within two weeks of each other and through divine intervention, I managed to pass both. I drove my cab back to the taxi garage and hopped another bus this time to my brother's apartment and took up residence on his convertible couch.

Forty years ago, it was much easier to accept cases on an assigned basis which is a procedure whereby you could make a living before you had established a paying clientele. Accepting cases on an assigned basis meant you would be paid by the city or state to represent indigents charged with criminal offenses. You'll remember Mr. Gideon in Florida. In the District of Columbia system, you could be assigned more serious cases almost immediately upon admission to the Bar. There was a waiting period commensurate with experience in New York. I was able to make a better living in Washington than New York at the beginning of my career as a criminal defense attorney.

One of the earliest cases assigned to me in Washington was a young black man charged with Pandering or being a pimp. Ricky Love was his nom de guerre. Ricky was more than handsome. He was pretty and intelligent and had talent as a fashion designer. He had established a modestly successful design business for a few years in the garment district of New York City. But he could not compete in the cut throat, Mafia dominated industry as it existed at that time and his business failed. Ricky returned to Washington after his business failed and began cultivating friendships in the escort service in his hometown. He was basically a hanger-on who aspired to the wealth and glamour of the call girl service industry. The service liked him because he could attract the most beautiful of women to their employ. Love was a promoter and not a purveyor of the sex. He was just earning a name for himself in the escort service industry in Washington but was stopped in his tracks when he was indicted for Pandering in the Superior Court of the District of Columbia.

I was assigned to represent Ricky Love in the District of Columbia which did him no real benefit because all the judges knew that I was from New York therefore I was a carpetbagger and Jewish. I had the look. Dark, curly hair, dark eyes and after all isn't everyone with that look and from New York, Jewish? That was the attitude of most of the judges I dealt with in the Superior Court with a few notable exceptions. Forty years ago, there was hardly any ethnicity in the District of Columbia. There were either black or Caucasians with northern European names. In actuality, I am a thoroughbred Sicilian with the ability to trace both sides of my family and surname to a small village a few kilometers from Agrigento. I felt the cynicism and condescension that I was an outsider whose physical features and ethnicity would never allow entrance into the closed family of Superior Court attorneys. I felt the sting of anti-Semitism without being Jewish. With that as my situation as a defender of the indigent in the Superior Court of the District of Columbia, I endeavored to represent Ricky Love, alleged panderer. I never mentioned to the Superior Court jurists that my ancestors had kicked the Sephardic Jews out of Sicily some five hundred years prior to my first appearance in their courtrooms.

Love was a cooperative client and certainly did not possess the personality traits you would associate with your average pimp. He dressed casually, had an engaging personality and was slight in build. I should imagine that if ever he was of a mind to use physical force to keep the women in line that he would be the loser as many of the women were taller and stronger than him. He used his looks and personality to gain traction in the escort business for, given his good looks, there would never be any need for brute force. As Love was building up a head of steam in his new endeavor, he made a trip to the Minneapolis-St. Paul area of Minnesota with the intention of finding young women who would be willing to serve as highly paid escorts in the Washington, D.C. area. Minnesota, in general, is a favored area to recruit young women willing to serve as escorts. The blond haired, blue eyed descendants of the original Nordic and Germanic settlers were highly prized by the escort services back east. There is an area on 8th avenue in Manhattan called the Minnesota strip because of the number of blond haired, blue eyed young prostitutes who ply their trade there.

Love never found any of the descendants of the original settlers but he did strike up a relationship with a very attractive young brunette in her early twenties who, as you might guess, worked on an occasional basis for the largest escort service in the Minneapolis-St. Paul area. Love managed to convince her that there was more money to be made in the District of Columbia as a full-time escort than as a part time one in the twin cities especially with him acting as her agent. After all, Ricky was as beautiful as her and had many associates in the business there. She was easily convinced of the economic potential of such an arrangement and quickly agreed to change her residence from the barren plains of Minneapolis-St. Paul to the fertile fields of our nation's capital awash in government money and horny politicians.

Ricky had been living at home with his parents before his trip to Minnesota. He also had an apartment in an upper middle class building on Massachusetts Avenue not all that far from the District of Columbia Superior Court an area which was to become all too familiar to him. Love sublet the apartment to various friends who would invariably abandon the apartment without paying the rent. High end escorts were never known to share their wealth with landlords or gullible subletors like Ricky Love. I have represented many drug dealers in the past who were making thousands of dollars per day selling drugs who would end up getting evicted from the apartments they rented where the drugs were packaged for failure to pay the rent. Most of them were living with their parents and the attitude was that the parents were responsible for the rent even though they were making enough money to buy the apartment building itself with cash. The same attitude prevailed in the escort business. Someone else would always be responsible for the rent. No overhead expenses for these pillars of the community. No sales tax either.

One fateful day Love decided to establish his business with his new partner in the aforementioned apartment on Massachusetts Avenue which was now vacant of tenants. You might say that Ricky's new partner had a hands-on approach to the business. Things were going along swimmingly at the apartment until Love's business partner from Minnesota got into a fight with another escort in the courtyard of the building and was stabbed. Although he would never confirm my suspicions, I suspected that the stabber was one of Ricky's old girlfriends and she was jealous of the arrangement between Ricky and his new business partner. Either that or it was a fight over turf where each of them could ply their trade. It was probably a combination of both. In any event, the incident led to a series of events which led to the destruction of Love's new business and eventual indictment.

Although seriously injured, the maiden from Minnesota recovered from her injuries. The police are required by law to be notified of such an assault. Any injury or death deemed by medical personnel to be suspicious in nature must be reported to the police. The maiden's injury was beyond suspicious. It was a felonious assault and the police were required to make further inquiry. Before the inquiry could get started, the stabber hired a well-known Washington attorney whose chief source of income was in the representation of prostitutes and their pimps. The attorney was instructed by the stabber and her business associates to make an offer to the Minnesota maiden to pay all her medical expenses along with several thousand dollars of walking around money if she would not press charges. He presented the maiden with an agreement which she signed. The attorney in question was very experienced and must have known that the mere suggestion of an offer of money in lieu of not pressing charges was, itself, a crime called Obstruction of Justice. He later told me that he regretted his decision to intercede on behalf of the stabber who was a steady client. Once a crime has been committed an agreement not to press charges does not make the crime evaporate into the atmosphere. The lawyer knew this and was very worried about being indicted himself and/or losing his license to practice law. He survived the ordeal and the case became so muddled that only one person was indicted. That's right, it was Ricky Love. Neither Ricky nor the indictment had anything to do with the assault or the agreement. The attorney of whom I speak later became a superior court judge. I should have had a practice like his.

It seems that the maiden from Minnesota told the United States Attorney that she was exactly that; a maiden before she met Ricky Love. He had lured her away from her job as a school teacher with the promise or fame and fortune in his fashion business in the District of Columbia. She told the prosecutor that upon arrival in D.C. she was shocked, do you hear, shocked to learn that the business was actually an escort business. Ricky had forced her to compromise her virtue and sense of morality and it was all his fault that she had gotten stabbed. I wondered if, as she was feeding this line of bullshit to the prosecutor, she felt more discomfort from the five hundred-dollar bills stuffed into her brasserie than from the untruths that came out of her mouth. A mouth which Ricky Love had insisted become part of her repertoire as a device to increase their profits.

The Minnesota maiden told the U.S. Attorney that she was a school teacher and a virgin before she fell in love with Ricky Love. This was not her idea of falling in love with love but that she had been seduced for the first time by Ricky's proclamation of love. Ricky Love and false love had destroyed her happy life in Minnesota. The U.S. Attorney bought her story of the defiled teacher of young children who was as pure as the newly driven snow before she met Ricky Love. The prosecutor did little or no investigation into these allegations of her life before she met and fell in love with Love. If he had, he would have quickly discovered that the Minnesota maiden was as pure as the newly driven slush. My apologies to the memory of the famous actress Tallulah Bankhead who has been given credit for coining the phrase when describing her lifestyle. It seems inconceivable that any relatively sophisticated prosecutor would assign any credibility to the maiden's fairy tale. Perhaps he thought that he would be the superhero who would save the damsel in distress or maybe he was simply under pressure from his superiors to make an example of Ricky. Whatever it was one thing was certain. Ricky Love was facing serious jail time if convicted.

I made the decision very early on that in order to save Ricky from becoming somebody's wife in prison it would be necessary to go to the twin cities area. Since I was assigned counsel, it would be necessary to obtain permission from the judge for the funds to make the trip. I was used to the New York system which meant that if a judge gave you his word that he would sign an order reimbursing you for your expenses you would get reimbursed. I did not realize that an attorney who was not homegrown in the District of Columbia system could be trifled with by the Superior Court judges. I told the judge that I would probably need only one weekend in Minneapolis-St. Paul to accomplish my task but it was absolutely necessary that my client accompany me. He agreed to reimburse me for all my expenses and Ricky's expenses so far as they were not extravagant. Taking the judge at his word was the first of many missteps I made during the representation of Ricky Love, my new travel companion.

I decided that we would need an experienced investigator to make the trip with us so I called upon my old paralegal buddy, Terry Lasky, who by this time has become a licensed investigator. The judge indicated that he would not allow reimbursement for an investigator especially one who licensed only in New York. I prevailed upon Terry to accept the promise of Ricky Love to reimburse him for expenses and pay him at his usual hourly rate reminding him of our recent success and windfall in the Etta James case. Terry agreed and on one very pleasant weekend in late autumn the three of us packed our bags and boarded a flight to Minneapolis.

We started our investigation in the red-light district of St. Paul. Love had received information from one of his friends in the business that the Minnesota maiden may have worked at a massage parlor in that area. We happened upon a likely establishment which advertised an Asian massage whatever the hell that was, but featured 8x10 glossies of your typical sorority sweethearts on the large billboards outside the entrance. When we walked through the door we soon discovered what an Asian massage was about. It started very quickly as we were greeted by the Asian proprietress who immediately demanded the fifty-dollar admission fee.

"You pay fifty dollar. You pay fifty dollar for massage" she shouted.

Her bedside manner left something to be desired. It led me to speculate as to the bedside manner we could expect upon payment of the required fee. We informed the proprietress that we wanted information not a massage. I was tempted to ask what an Asian massage was, but I soon realized that there was failure of communication between me and the proprietress who was only interested in the fifty-dollar fee. I showed her a photo of the maiden and asked if she knew her.

"You want special girl for maybe hand job? Cost you hundred dollar. No money, no hand job."

I responded. I all but shoved the photo in her face and said, "You know girl, right?" Mimicking her foreign accent and broken English. This seemed to really piss her off. Now she was screaming at us in a language which seemed to be a cross between an unknown language and English. We understood only that the price of admission was now one hundred dollars apiece. I kept waving the photo in front of her when she suddenly turned away from us and started shouting to someone in a back room. A few seconds later, the figure of an Asian man the size of a sumo wrestler appeared a few feet in front of us. His arms were the size of a Japanese maple tree and they were outstretched in front of him, pointed in our direction. By this time the proprietress and the sumo wrestler were screaming at us in their respective native languages which we understood to mean that we had better get our asses out of there, pronto. We ran out the front door with the sumo wrestler in hot pursuit in an attempt to reach the alleged safety of our rental vehicle which was only about one half the size of our new friend chasing us down the street. It was fortunate that we got away. Our little rental car would have been no match for the sumo wrestler.

Ricky had told us that the maiden had worked at other massage parlors in the area but my instinct told me that we would achieve similar results in those places as well. So, we decided to visit some of the bars that were frequented by working girls and their customers. These bars featured nude dancing in glass enclosed stages and large screen football games on the many televisions surrounding the bar area. The city fathers must have realized that liquor and nude dancing don't mix so they proclaimed that the dancing and the drinking should be completely separated while the customers were able to enjoy both views. There was even a separate entrance to the enclosed stage area giving the effect of attached but separate buildings. In legal jargon, you could say that the entrances were separate but equal. It was the height of college football season when we visited this bar so most of the patrons were watching television while the nude dancers labored virtually unnoticed.

We had chosen this particular bar as our first stop because we had heard that the Minnesota maiden liked to bounce checks in this establishment. Since bartenders seem to know most of their clientele, Terry and I devised a stratagem designed to coax information from the bartender. But as soon as we mentioned the maiden's name, the bartender opened his cash register and handed us two cancelled checks endorsed by the maiden and marked insufficient funds. It usually consumes a great deal of time to extract information from witnesses most of whom do not want to get involved. Not only was the bartender cooperative but he volunteered that he would be happy to be a witness against the Minnesota maiden if needed. Then he gave us a lead as to a couple of other bars which had suffered the same fate as his establishment as a result of trusting the maiden. We quickly went over to these places and were given two more bounced checks endorsed by the maiden almost without asking. The cooperative bartender at the first place had placed a few unsolicited calls to his friends at the other establishments and they were waiting for us when we arrived. When we completed our mission at the bars, we had five bounced checks and two witnesses who were willing to testify that not only was the school teacher story a fable but the maiden had a predilection for supplementing her night job by bouncing checks during the day.

We had completed most of our business in less time than it would take one of the bar patrons to finish watching a college football game, but we still needed a witness who had firsthand knowledge of the maiden's life as an escort.

For that purpose, we turned to Ricky Love himself. It was getting late in the afternoon on Saturday and we had less than one day to locate and interview these witnesses. So, we went back to the hotel where Love started calling his friends some of whom might have been customers of the maiden. We arranged a meeting with one of them who indicated that he knew the maiden as an escort without indicating how he knew. More importantly, he told us about a party in Minneapolis at the apartment of the best-known madam in the twin cities who ran the largest escort service in the area. Through Love's friend, we managed to get ourselves invited to the party. The friend indicated that the madam and most of the escorts in attendance probably knew the maiden. We showed up at the appointed time and were introduced to the madam and many of her friends. Most of them did not look or act like escorts but we did not know how escorts were supposed to act when not on a business call. They seemed like ordinary party goers until you struck up a conversation with one of them. It was a mixed crowd and the party seemed to be an excellent vehicle for networking, if you get my drift.

We fanned out and tried to speak with as many party goers as possible. At one point, I found myself dancing with the madam herself. I assumed the traditional dance position with the madam but she was having nothing to do with my arm around her waist. She knocked my arm off her waist which left it dangling at my side during the entire dance. That left us dancing hand to hand rather than cheek to cheek. She used her free arm to thwart any attempt to reposition my arm and I joked that we had just invented a new dance step. The madam did not react to my feeble attempt at humor. She remained stone faced but you could not help but notice the faux diamond earrings shaped like dollar signs dangling from her ears. Her looks were pleasant enough but she was not all that attractive and was a bit on the plump side having grown fat, I would imagine, on the riches of her lucrative business. She did tell me that she knew the Minnesota maiden but could not remember whether she had worked for her as an escort. We got the names of a few people who knew the Minnesota maiden better than the madam was willing to say, interviewed them either at the party or the next day just before we left the twin cities. Two of those witnesses were willing to testify against the maiden making a total of four and between them and the bounced checks. I was loaded for bear when I got back to Washington.

A few days later I walked into the office of U.S Attorney, threw the bounced checks on his desk and proclaimed that his complainant was nothing but a thief who spent most of her young adult life in Minnesota teaching the fine art of being a successful courtesan rather than molding young minds. I then gave him the names and numbers of the establishments from where I had procured the fraudulent checks. I also told him about the witnesses who were willing to testify on my client's behalf. Finally, I told him about the party thrown by the president of the largest escort service in the twin cities and finished the conversation by asking him if he liked to dance. I told him to check out my information and that I would contact him again in two weeks' time. I suggested a plea of guilty to a misdemeanor and no jail time for Ricky Love. He never answered my question about dancing but I was ready, willing and able to teach him some new steps.

Before I had a chance to contact the assistant U.S. Attorney for his answer to my proposal, Love announced that I was no longer his attorney. Love, who was supposed to be without funds to hire an attorney to represent him, engaged one of the highest priced criminal defense attorneys in Washington. In that case when you are replaced by another attorney, you are required to cooperate with that attorney. There is generally no acrimony between attorneys unless your ex-client owed you money. Then things could get a little sticky. Since I was an assigned attorney, Ricky owed me no money and the code of ethics would forbid me to accept money from any other source but the District of Columbia. Most importantly, you are to act in a professional manner at all times.

I turned over my file to the new attorney but refrained from telling him about most of our activities in Minneapolis-St. Paul. When the new attorney failed to make inquiry about our trip, Ricky asked me to oversee his case. Love made the mistake of asking me in person. Calling upon all the professionalism I could muster, I told Love that the only thing I would oversee would be his useless ass exiting my office. I then told him that he was an ungrateful jerk and a real asshole for making a mockery of my sacred duty to zealously defend him. He showed no emotion when I informed him that the judge had played me for a sucker also by changing his mind about reimbursement which meant that my out of pocket expenses would be a total loss and I would not be paid for the hours of work running around the twin cities on his behalf. He did give me money for Terry's bill, in cash. I finally pointed to the door and told him to remove his girlish body from the premises and to never contact me again for any reason. I never saw him again. My labor for Love was lost as was my money. After suffering that kind of abuse, I decided that the case of the United States v. Ricky Love would be my last in the District of Columbia. I gave up my office in Washington and returned to New York City.

VI. His Vision Of Reality
Was Not At All Like Ours:
The Midtown Slasher

One of the first murder cases that I tried involved a long forgotten serial killer named Joseph Christopher. Christopher was a racist psychopath who preyed exclusively on Afro-Americans or men he perceived as Afro-Americans. Joseph Christopher was as grave a threat to black men both young and old that has existed in the past half century. He was born and raised in small town a few miles outside of Buffalo, New York where he wantonly murdered eight black men in 1980. He was also accused of killing two black men in nearby Rochester and on December 22, 1980, he shut down the center of Manhattan with a killing spree that had no equal. On that date, the bodies of four black men appeared in rapid succession on the streets of Manhattan. The upper east side, the lower west side, Madison Avenue and Penn Station were all sites of dead black men who had been stabbed through the heart. The police set up road blocks, stopped the trains from leaving Penn Station and Grand Central and slowed subway traffic to a crawl. Two additional stabbings occurred in the same time frame with no fatalities. One on a subway coming from Queens and the other in the garment district. The police were in a quandary as they raced from one scene to the other. The reports came in rapid succession stretching police personnel to its breaking point. When the newspapers got wind of this they immediately dubbed the stabber as the "Midtown Slasher."

Joseph Gerard Christopher was born and raised in Lockport, New York. His upbringing seemed uneventful until his father died of cancer when Christopher was a young teenager. His father had a hunting cabin in that area where he taught his son the use of rifles and pistols both of which were in abundance at the cabin. Christopher seemed like a normal kid growing up until his father died then his personality changed. He graduated from high school and held down jobs as a laborer and maintenance man in the Buffalo area. One of those jobs was as an orderly in a hospital where he befriended an Afro-American man who was a maintenance man at the hospital. They remained friends through the duration of Christopher's employment at the hospital. He had a sister who, during this time, became engaged to an Afro-American man who may have been a friend of Christopher's hospital friend. When her engagement was announced he severed his friendship with his hospital buddy and became more reclusive spending much of his time at his father's now unused cabin in the woods. There he could be alone with his thoughts which, as history has taught us, grew increasingly psychotic. His mother was of Italian heritage and as an American basically raised in a household which featured the Italian language and social mores, I can speculate that the virulent racism displayed by Christopher may have had its roots in his own household as a child. Italians in Italy are very tolerant but when they come to the United States, their attitudes change and blacks are vilified and became the butt of crude jokes.

Alone in the cabin Christopher began to tinker with his father's weapons. He sawed off the barrels of at least two of his father's .22 caliber rifles and sanded down the insides of what was left of the barrels. Each weapon has a unique set of whirls called rifling. These whirls help guide the projectile or bullet through the barrel and out the muzzle on its way to the target. Rifling leaves a unique mark on the projectile which can be traced to an individual weapon. This was Christopher's attempt to destroy the marks on any bullet which would be fired from those .22 rifles. He adjusted the trigger mechanism on the rifles so they would fire at a more rapid rate and fine-tuned the length of the barrels so the entire weapon could fit into a medium sized brown paper bag and under his jacket. One fine night in the spring of 1980, Joseph Gerard Christopher took up one of his father's modified weapons, placed it in a brown paper bag, tucked it under his coat and headed out to the streets of Buffalo to begin a reign of terror which would last more than six months.

Christopher's modus operandi in Buffalo was different than in New York. In Buffalo, he used the modified .22 rifle to blow holes in the upper torso of his victims usually the head. Christopher would run up to his victims, pull the bag from under his jacket, take the rifle out of the bag and fire point blank into the head of his victim. The attacks were completely at random. Most times the victims never knew what hit them. Christopher usually wore the same type of clothing and he was described by a few eyewitnesses as a white male in his early twenties wearing wire rimmed glasses and a trench coat. They described the brown paper bag and Christopher's actions in pulling the weapon from the bag and firing. When I was preparing for trial in New York, I had to read the transcripts Christopher's earlier trial in Buffalo. One of his homicides involved the murder of a young black man, really only a kid, who was sitting in the front passenger seat of a parked car. It was witnessed by a nurse named Madonna Gorny who remembered seeing the young black man's head smoking as the bullet entered his right temple area.

The police in Buffalo did not realize that they were dealing with a serial killer until they started to match up the homicides with the witnesses' descriptions of Christopher and the similar manner in which the homicides were carried out. Up until that time, they had thought each of the homicides stood alone, unconnected to each other. By that time, three or four of the eight black men had been killed in rapid succession in different parts of the city. During this period of time, the police were also investigating the murders of two Afro-American cabdrivers whose throats had been cut and hearts cut out and bodies stuffed into the trunks. The cabs were found in remote parts of the city. The throat wounds were unique and seemed to have been made by the same weapon. In the same way, an elderly black man had his throat cut with a similar weapon while he was lying in a bed in the same hospital in which Christopher had worked. After Christopher had been captured, the Buffalo police conducted a thorough search of his father's cabin where they discovered several hunting knives which could inflict such damage. Christopher was never charged with those murders but the Buffalo police suspected that he was responsible for each of them. Judging by his acumen with knives in New York City on December 22, 1980, I would imagine their suspicions were accurate.

The reign of terror stopped as suddenly as it had begun. It had started in the late spring of 1980 and stopped by the early fall. You'll have to remember that we are dealing with Buffalo where the snows end in late spring and start up again in October. Christopher would have run the risk of the weapon malfunctioning in the cold or getting stuck in the snow as he made his escape. If you think I'm being facetious, then you've never been to that part of New York State when the earth tilts away from the sun and the days grow short. In fact, Christopher had joined the army and been sent to Fort Benning, Georgia for training. He must have finished first in his class at the firing range and use of the bayonet. There was some speculation that he had enlisted because things were beginning to heat up for him in Buffalo and he needed to hide somewhere in plain sight. Whatever the reason, Christopher decided to visit New York City during the Christmas holidays in 1980 while on leave from his duty station at Fort Benning.

Hiding in plain sight is more easily accomplished in the biggest city in the United States. Christopher arrived in New York a couple of days before his killing spree. He holed up in one of many fleabag hotels that proliferated the Times Square area. It was called the National Hotel and was located on 7th Avenue just around the corner from 42nd Street. The National was a haven for murder, mayhem, prostitution and drug dealing. During the few days in which Christopher had taken up residence at the National, he remained virtually unnoticed amid the turmoil. He would save his misanthropy for the crowded boulevards of New York City where everyone could see and appreciate his artistry.

Christopher warmed to his task by doing what good Christians would do in celebration of the birth of Christ. He went to church and prayed to the almighty for guidance. To say that Christopher was dangerously psychotic would be a gross understatement. He prayed to the Protestant God at the Marble Collegiate Church and to the Catholic God at St. Patrick's Cathedral located nearby on 5th Avenue. The voices told him to pray to God. He was pleased to learn that the Lord was in agreement with him that he should continue the killing spree in New York that began in Buffalo. He went back to the National hotel, fortified himself with a meal, tucked his knife into his winter jacket and went out to commit mayhem.

After the killing spree, Christopher disappeared. The police organized a group of detectives specially formed to solve the case. That task force of detectives really did not know where to start. Christopher had left no evidence behind. The police had a general description of him but there was nothing out of the ordinary about those descriptions. They investigated every guest who had occupied a room in all of the rundown single occupancy hotels that proliferated the midtown area during that period of time. A Herculean task that yielded no leads. The police paperwork of this part of the investigation took up a small room in the office of the District Attorney. I went through about half of it but realized that most of it was only a record of the continuing police frustration with their inability to develop leads.

After about a month and one half of dead ends, the real break in the case came from Christopher himself. He had returned to his duty station at Fort Benning but he was even more dangerous than he was in Buffalo or New York. Upon his return to duty, he discovered that his new bunk mate was a young black man. Christopher heard the voice of God commanding him to continue his holy crusade against the Afro-American race and one day when his bunk mate turned his back, Christopher plunged a knife into him. There was no problem identifying Christopher as the culprit. He did it in front of other members of his platoon and the bunk mate was able to tell the military police who had done it. Christopher had murdered four men in front of the multitudes in New York and was easily able to escape into the crowd. In Buffalo, he escaped into the night. His psychosis had become so profound that there was no thought of escape at Fort Benning.

Christopher was being held in the brig at Fort Benning awaiting formal charges for the assault on his bunk mate when he attempted suicide. It was really a halfhearted attempt more in the nature of a cry for help. In recognition of the name the New York press had bestowed upon him, he slashed his wrists. The wounds were easily treated and he was placed under the care of an army psychiatrist whom I later called as a witness at Christopher's murder trial in New York. The army psychiatrist was female and white and she had developed a rapport with him. Christopher revealed more about his racist homicidal compulsions to her than to any of the myriad of psychiatrists who would come to examine him. This was why her testimony would become critical to the defense. When he was a patient in the psych ward at the army hospital he came under the care of a psychiatric male nurse named Anderson. He was assigned to assist Christopher on a daily basis. It was to Anderson that Christopher began speaking of the reign of terror in Buffalo.

I have discovered, in the course of four decades of dealing with dangerous psychopaths like Christopher, almost everyone of them wants to relieve themselves of the weight of guilt which burdens their soul. Somewhere in the deep recesses of their unfathomable lack of feeling for their fellow man, there exists a spark of genuine humanity. Joseph Christopher was a homicidal racist who couldn't give a damn about his victims. He swore allegiance to the voice of God which commanded him to go forth to rid the world of the black race but there invariably comes a day of reckoning. That day of reckoning was at hand and his confessor was army nurse Anderson.

Christopher began to speak of the murders in Buffalo in general terms never indicating to Anderson that he was the guilty party. Anderson grew suspicious of Christopher's third person characterizations and asked why Christopher would talk about his hometown when the crime for which he was charged occurred in Georgia. Anderson's questions grew more specific and Christopher began to fill in the details of his murder spree. There was some indication that Christopher thought that the fellow soldier he had attacked may have been from Buffalo which may have touched off his homicidal attack. Anderson quickly realized the gravity of Christopher's oblique references to the Buffalo murders and in a short period of time, Christopher made some very incriminating statements about his Christmas holiday in New York City also. Anderson continued his sessions with Christopher after his commanding officer had been notified who, in turn, had notified the authorities in Buffalo and New York City but Christopher was not as forthcoming as he was on the occasion of his initial confession. When law enforcement authorities attempted to interview him, he said nothing. I learned a few years later that silence would be the response to my questions also.

Christopher was tried for the murders in Buffalo before the murders in New York City. When he was tried in Buffalo he had already been in jail for two years. He was convicted of at least three of the murders and received a sentence of a minimum of sixty-five years and a maximum of life. Christopher's lawyers in Buffalo realized that he was legally insane and not competent to stand trial. The legal standard for incompetency is the lack of understanding of the nature of the proceedings against the accused along with the inability to cooperate with his counsel because of his mental infirmity. Plenty of my clients have refused to cooperate with me because it was in their nature not to cooperate. It is the difference between a personality disorder and a true psychosis which had consumed Joseph Christopher.

The judge before whom Christopher was tried in Buffalo gave no credence to his lawyer's demands for a competency examination and he was tried without any real knowledge of whether Christopher was able to understand the nature of the proceedings against him. The appellate court reversed Christopher's convictions because the trial judge had not ordered a competency examination as requested by his attorneys. By this time nearly three years had passed since Christopher had first been arrested. It was agreed that he would be sent to New York City to stand trial for the murder spree on December 22, 1980 before he was retried for the Buffalo murders.

It was now 1983 and while I remembered Christopher's reign of terror in Manhattan in 1980, I was also able to recall the exact date because it was my birthday. I did not have the least notion that he would one day become my client. Joseph Christopher's case was among the very first of its kind to be prosecuted in Manhattan at that time. While there were other serial killers brought to justice, none had the blatant racial overtones as did the Christopher case. The case against David Berkowitz, the son of Sam, comes to mind. The fact that Christopher's murders happened on one day and during only a few hours of that day and then stopped completely lent it a surreal character. The powers that be decided that the defense of Joseph Christopher should be assigned to the New York University Criminal Law Clinic. That choice was as demented as Joseph Christopher was psychotic. So, began the defense's trip to never land from which, as the word suggests, it would never recover.

The NYU Criminal Law Clinic was designed to provide third year law students with some practical experience in representing those charged with minor crimes in an actual courtroom setting. The clinic is usually directed by an attorney with courtroom experience and a knowledge of the criminal court process. In this case, I was familiar with the director having worked with him when I was a paralegal for the Legal Aid Society. He was a good enough attorney but he had an ego which ran afoul of prosecutors, judges, courtroom staff and fellow attorneys or anyone else who got in his way. I could imagine him lobbying to be assigned to the case with his inexhaustible supply of photocopiers and bright, dedicated but horribly inexperienced students.

Christopher shuttled between Buffalo and New York City for about two years before he was tried in Buffalo. This permitted the case in New York to dispense with many preliminary matters which would have taken up an extra couple of years or so if that agreement had not been reached between the prosecuting agencies. You'll remember that the law clinic was designed to handle minor offenses such as misdemeanors, violations, traffic tickets and the like. Here it was assigned the monumental task of defending a serial killer with absolutely no knowledge or experience of how to proceed. I don't believe that the egotistical director of the clinic had ever tried a homicide case. He had worked for the Legal Aid Society which at that time was not permitted to represent those charged with murder. What was the leadership of the defense bar thinking when they permitted the NYU clinic to be solely responsible for a case which required so much more? I shall be brief in describing the missteps.

The law students worked tirelessly on behalf of Christopher, but because they had such poor leadership they were misdirected to research irrelevant issues. During my one and only meeting with the director of the clinic, he spoke glowingly of his students in unearthing the Posse Comitatus Act of 1879 which basically restricted the federal government from using military personnel acting as domestic law enforcement personnel. The Act was passed by Congress in 1879 to remove the occupying Union troops from southern states after Reconstruction. What the hell did Posse Comitatus have to do with the defense of a psychotic, racist serial killer? You'll remember that Christopher was arrested by military police but for a crime committed while he was in the military. The U.S. Army certainly had the authority to make the arrest. When he was turned over to the civilian authorities in New York, the military charges were still pending and it was at the discretion of the military to do so. Fodder for an academic discussion but as a theory in defense of Christopher? I think not.

The real reason the NYU clinic was relieved of its responsibilities and I was assigned can be attributed to a conflict which had arisen between the director and Christopher not to mention my affinity to attract the most psychologically unbalanced of clients. It might be an understatement to say that as part of his mental condition, Christopher was above all paranoid. If memory serves me correctly, the director of the clinic had made some irresponsible promises to Christopher about the success of his defensive strategy. A competency hearing was held in front of an Afro-American judge after the case had been sent there by a supervising Afro-American judge. Coincidentally I had been just sent to this particular judge for trial in a rape case but was, just as quickly, sent to another judge as Christopher's case replaced mine. At that time, I had no idea that I would eventually represent Christopher but I remember the incident vividly. At that hearing the clinic engaged the services of the late Dr. John Train an eminent psychiatrist well respected in his field. The prosecution countered with a psychiatric social worker who was a hired gun for the prosecution. Dr. Train said that not only was Christopher not competent to stand trial but his murderous rage could have been the result of mental illness. The psychiatric social worker said that the uncontrollable impulses to kill only Afro-Americans not to mention Christopher's direct communications with the Lord were the result of depression and that Christopher's behavior was merely a symptom of that diagnosis. It was a battle of the experts. One with a long history in forensics and an elected diplomat in the Society of Forensic Psychiatry and the other who had a master's degree in social work with no known noteworthy achievements in the field. In front of an Afro-American judge, you can guess what happened.

Growing bored with the defense of Joseph Christopher especially after he had lost the competency hearing, the director of the clinic created a problem that could have easily been avoided. Whatever transpired between the director of the NYU clinic, the students and Christopher, it became increasing obvious that Christopher's mental condition had worsened. He began writing letters to the judge that he would refuse to eat because he believed his food was being poisoned by his attorney. Instead of requesting another mental competency examination, the director of the clinic used his client's accusations as a reason to get excused from any further representation of Christopher. I believed that the NYU clinic used their representation of Christopher as a vehicle for academic inquiry. When he had outlived his usefulness, they dropped him and left the case a total disaster.

I picked up the file from the NYU Clinic the same day as I learned about Posse Comitatus. I really did not know where to start. The file was replete with academic discussions of legal insanity, applicable law and criminal procedure. I suspect that the discussions on criminal procedure had to do more with informing the students than formulating a defense for Christopher. There were indecipherable notes, random case law, and a copy of school quiz but no indication as to the direction of the defense. There were copies of letters written by Christopher to the presiding judge about his belief that his lawyer was poisoning his food and his dissatisfaction with his lawyer's efforts on his behalf. Those letters seemed to be an indication of his contempt for the criminal justice system in New York City. In Buffalo, he had cooperated with his lawyers and did not seem to exhibit the same contempt.

When I first interviewed Christopher he refused to speak with me. He told me to go talk to the wall. Those were the only words Christopher would utter in my presence during entire two-and-one-half-year period that I represented him. Christopher was being held in several maximum-security prisons during the pre-trial phase of his incarceration. Those prisons featured the most secure facilities for those inmates like Christopher who needed to be separated from the general population. If he were allowed into the general population, it would be a certainty that he would have run amuck with the majority black inmate population. The black population would have certainly targeted him and he would have never survived.

One of those maximum-security prisons was in a small city located in the heart of the Finger Lakes area of New York State called Auburn. Auburn Prison has a long history of existence going back to the early19th century and was written about by a visiting French historian the Marquis de Tocqueville. At that time Auburn was the epitome of the reform movement in prisons but by the end of the 19th century, it was the place of the first electrocution in the United States. Christopher was housed there during most of the period of his pre-trial incarceration. I know a lot about the prison because I was born and raised only a few city blocks from the prison. I used to play hand ball with my friends against the prison walls in my youth. The prison is right out of a James Cagney movie with enormously high prison walls and guard towers at the top of each corner of the prison which overlook the entire prison area. The prison itself takes up a large portion of the center of the city. It was the "Big House" or "going up the river" the terms used by the actors in the famous prison movies of the 1930s, only in Auburn, it was going up one of the Finger Lakes. Little did I know that when I was growing up in the shadow of the prison that I would spent my adult life helping to populate it or visiting a psychotic serial killer like Joseph Christopher.

When I took over the case, Christopher had ceased communication with everyone except the voices in his head. On several occasions, I would travel to my hometown to visit Christopher. I visited my parents, aunts, uncles, cousins and friends but never Christopher himself. I would go to the prison, sign in as his attorney and ask to visit with him. On each of those occasions, he would refuse. I asked to be allowed to talk at him in a room, but if a prisoner does not give you permission to visit with him, then there is nothing the prison officials could do to accommodate you. One of the deputy wardens was a friend from high school, but he could do nothing for me. When Christopher was transported to New York City for his court appearances, I was able to talk at him in the holding cells but he would never respond. There was no question that the director of the student law clinic at NYU had done irreparable damage to Christopher's case.

The single most important consequence of Christopher's uncooperative attitude was his failure to cooperate with the psychiatrists I had engaged to examine him. I was caught in a dilemma. I knew that he was psychotic and probably not responsible for his actions. But, in order for a jury to consider such a defense, you must tell them that your client actually committed the murders for which he was charged but that he was not responsible because of mental disease or defect. The law defining not guilty by reason of insanity was promulgated in England in 1843 and known as the McNaughton rule and is still the standard to this day in New York. The defense must show that his client did not know right from wrong and could not appreciate the consequences of his actions. It is a very difficult standard to prove to a jury and you must get an expert to express his professional opinion that the standard had been met to get it into evidence for a jury to consider. In 1980 when the murders were committed, if an insanity defense was interposed, it would be the burden of the prosecution to prove that the defendant was sane at the time of the commission of the offense. The law as to the burden of prove was shifted to the defense a few years later after the prosecution failed to prove John Hinckley was sane in the attempted assassination of Ronald Reagan. In reality, it was always the actual burden of the defense to prove insanity, if not the legal burden.

When it became clear that Christopher was never going to communicate with me or anyone else for that matter, I had to decide as to which defense would be plausible under the circumstances. It was vitally necessary that

Christopher speak with another psychiatrist if I was going to have any success with an insanity defense. Since he would not speak at all, I was left with the defense of making the prosecution prove their case beyond a reasonable doubt which is what the prosecution must do in any case. I was faced with the Hobson's choice letting the jury know that Christopher was a crazed killer and trying to prove he was insane or saying nothing to the jury as to a defense which is any defendant's right, and then letting the prosecution prove its case. If, by some miracle, Christopher were free to roam the streets again without treatment, he would continue to be a grave threat to society especially to those who were dark skinned. Any black man or Caucasian who had just returned from the beach with a deep tan could become the target of Christopher's murderous intent as was the case in New York City when the only murder for which Christopher was convicted involved a dark skinned Hispanic. He could not tell the difference and probably did not care. The only hope for Christopher to redeem his life was to undergo intensive psychiatric treatment in the only place where he could receive it, a hospital for the criminally insane. I opted for an insanity defense and thought of a way to prove it with or without his cooperation.

Christopher was suspected of four murders and two attempted murders during his Christmas spree in New York City but he was indicted for only one of the murders and one of the attempted murders. The persons who witnessed the other three murders and the second victim who was stabbed but survived could not identify Christopher at a lineup conducted by the office of the District Attorney. The District Attorney declined to prosecute in those cases because they had no other evidence connecting him to those attacks. I have been present at many lineups in my career but the lineup conducted in Christopher's case was the best I have ever experienced. Each individual in the lineup was a white male almost exactly the same height and weight and about the same age as Christopher who also was in the lineup. All of them wore wire rimmed glasses and baseball caps which was Christopher's choice of apparel when he went on the murder spree. In the present day, you could say that the five other participants in the lineup were clones of Christopher.

It was now the spring of 1985 and Christopher had been in jail for nearly five consecutive years. I had been on the case for about two years and was getting bi-weekly phone calls from Jim Fogel, the prosecutor as to when I would be ready for trial. Jim was a very knowledgeable District Attorney and a formidable adversary. He was also very understanding as I explained to him the total mess the NYU clinic had made of the case and Christopher's subsequent complete lack of cooperation. I had filed a notice of intent to interpose a defense of not responsible because of mental disease or defect as the statute required. The notice put the Office of the District Attorney on notice that the defense intended to present expert witness testimony as to Christopher's mental state at the time of the commission of the offenses. The District Attorney would then have the right to have Christopher examined by one of their psychiatrists. But since Christopher would not speak to anyone, it would have been a waste of time and money for them to arrange such an interview. Fogel must have wondered where the hell I was coming from when I filed the notice. I was happy to learn that Fogel was not going to use the services of the same psychiatric social worker I spoke of earlier. In casual conversation with said social worker who was a fixture at the criminal court, he told me that when he interviewed Christopher in preparation for the competency hearing one of the conditions he had set for agreeing to the interview was that he had to be sure that there were "no niggers in the building." Even though I was admitting to the jury that my client was guilty of the murders, I did not want such a statement to come out on the record and in front of the jury. It was one thing to tell the jury that your client was a psychotic racist but an entirely different matter to hear it from his mouth.

The trial finally started in September of 1985. My plan was to call five witnesses for the defense. All of them were psychiatrists who had interviewed Christopher when he was willing to talk during the period between 1980 up until I came into the picture in 1983. Four of them were what are called fact witnesses and even though they were all expert witnesses who would be allowed to express their professional opinion, they could not in this instance because they had been used as expert witnesses as to Christopher's competency to stand trial and did not have enough information to form an opinion as to criminal responsibility. Since Christopher had stopped communicating altogether, when I set up appointments for them to interview him, he refused.

The first witness for the defense was the previously mentioned female psychiatrist who was still in the army when I contacted her. I had to clear her appearance with her commanding officer at Fort Benning who informed me that she would not be allowed to testify if she were asked her professional opinion as to criminal responsibility. I assured him that her testimony would be used only to lay a fact pattern as to what Christopher had revealed to her five years earlier when he confided in her the reasons for the attacks. In substance, he told her that the voices were in communication with God and that God had told the voices to tell him to go forth and kill black people. Her testimony ended there. I did not ask her opinion as to criminal responsibility. I remember meeting her at LaGuardia Airport and traveling with her to the hotel in the north tower of the World Trade Center which was the second one to fall on the same day sixteen years later. I also remember having lunch with her on the plaza below the hotel where many of the bodies of the desperate souls who chose this form of death rather than being burned alive by molten jet fuel on that infamous day had landed.

The second and third psychiatrists had been engaged by the NYU Clinic and were also fact witnesses who corroborated the army psychiatrist's testimony. The fourth psychiatrist was Dr. John Train. He went a bit further with his evaluation of Christopher's mental state. Dr. Train believed that Christopher was not competent to stand trial and had testified to same at the competency hearing a couple of years earlier. He was permitted to give his opinion as to his diagnosis of Paranoid Schizophrenia with homicidal ideation. But, like the others, he did not have enough information to form an opinion as to Christopher's state of mind at the time of the commission of the murders. Ordinarily upon the conclusion of a witnesses' testimony, no words are exchanged between the attorney and the witness as he leaves the stand but when a witness with the reputation and professional status of John Train pays you a compliment as he leaves the stand, it is a real honor. Dr. Train bent over as he passed me and whispered that I had asked some very good questions and that I had made an excellent record.

The fifth and final witness was Dr. Brian Joseph from Buffalo. He had been referred to me by Christopher's attorney in Buffalo. Dr. Joseph had done an evaluation of Christopher five years earlier but was not allowed to testify because the judge in Buffalo did not permit any psychiatric testimony at the trial in Buffalo. That erroneous ruling by the judge led to the reversal of the Buffalo convictions. Dr. Joseph could not render an opinion based upon his evaluation of Christopher but he could render an opinion based upon the record made of the four psychiatrists who had preceded him. Joseph Christopher did not know right from wrong nor did he understand or appreciate the consequences of his actions. Jim Fogel rose to object then paused briefly and stated that all the reasons upon which Dr. Joseph had based his opinion were legitimately in evidence and sat down without objecting. Dr. Joseph's testimony had saved the day for the defense. The possibility of a verdict of not responsible by reason mental disease or defect had become a reality.

Jim Fogel called about twenty-five witnesses. Most of them were police officers who testified as to their roles in the apprehension and gathering of evidence against Christopher. The critical witnesses were a young secretary who was just walking out of her office building on Madison Avenue for her lunch hour and the victim of the attempted murder both of whom had looked Christopher right in the eye when he wielded his knife. Anderson, the army nurse also testified. I had been advised by Christopher's Buffalo attorney that Anderson was a very nice guy and it turned out that his testimony was actually sympathetic but also damning against Christopher. The trial took about a month and I should note that it took about three days to pick a jury. I was limited by statute to twenty peremptory challenges. Those are challenges which require no reason to strike a prospective juror. I used most of them to strike every Afro-American who was questioned during jury selection. Jim Fogel knew what I was doing but never objected. Upon the conclusion of this process, Joseph Christopher would have his fate determined by an all-white jury.

The most dramatic part of the trial was the testimony of a young secretary who worked in a building on Madison Avenue around thirty-fifth street. She was just leaving the building for her lunch hour when she saw Christopher plunge a knife into the heart of Luis Rodriguez. Rodriguez was a dark skinned Hispanic but Christopher saw only dark skin and that set him off. Rodriguez was a bike messenger who had made a stop and was unlocking his bike when Christopher struck. The secretary had a side view of the murder but she was only a few feet away. She looked Christopher straight in the eye as he turned to make his escape. Rodriguez collapsed and died on the sidewalk a few seconds after the knife had torn through his heart. He was not Christopher's only victim. The young secretary had endured such emotional trauma that for several years after the incident she was still receiving therapy. Judging from the way in which she testified, I am sure that her recovery would be painstakingly slow and perhaps last a lifetime.

When the secretary walked through the well of the courtroom to the stand to testify, she never looked in Christopher's direction. Her gait was unbending and with a death-masked look on her face. I have been the part of many murder trials in my long career and have witnessed a lot of excruciatingly painful testimony but I will never forget the look of absolute terror on the secretary's face as she began her testimony. She never looked in Christopher's direction and she never took her eyes off Jim Fogel during direct testimony. She seemed to have been visualizing the words as they formed on his lips. When asked to make a courtroom identification of Christopher, her face turned pale. It took her a few seconds to compose herself then she moved her eyes to the left to where Christopher was sitting turning her head in his direction only enough to see him without having to look directly into his eyes. Throughout her entire testimony, it was obvious that she was as terrified to be in Christopher's presence at the trial as she had been for those few terrifying moments on Madison Avenue in December 1980.

The young witness went on to testify that she had suffered such great psychological trauma over the incident that she had repressed it far back into her memory that it took several sessions of hypnosis to bring it to the surface. I objected to her testimony but the judge overruled me. After Christopher had been convicted I filed a motion with the Appellate Division to have the appeals bureau of the Legal Aid Society assigned to handle his appeal. I did so because I knew Christopher would not make the effort himself and I wanted an experienced staff to look for legal error especially concerning the issue of hypnosis. What I got was an argument to the appeals court that Christopher had received ineffective assistance of counsel because I had used the insanity defense instead of letting the District Attorney prove the murders. I admit that the argument could be made that I was ineffective but the staff attorney who argued the case made no mention of hypnosis which was a far stronger argument. That was the last time I ever asked for the Legal Aid Society to be assigned to one of my clients. It was the difference between the mindset of an institutional defender and one who was free to make his own mistakes.

The second witness was an Afro-American man named Ivan Frasier who had looked Christopher straight in the eye and was easily able to identify him in the courtroom. Fraiser was riding a subway from Queens to Manhattan on the day he was attacked by Christopher. He testified that he noticed a young white male sitting across the aisle from him. Christopher was facing him and the reason Frasier remembered Christopher's facial features was because Christopher made a memorable display of a smile and direct eye contact when a pretty girl passed between them. In fact, Christopher had made it a point to attract Frasier's attention by rolling his eyes when the pretty girl had passed. Frasier was reading a newspaper when he noticed Christopher's actions and grinned back at him. It was the silent symbiosis of two healthy males appreciating the momentary sex appeal of a beautiful female. However briefly, Christopher was attempting to subliminally convince Frasier that he was just one of the guys.

Frasier repositioned the newspaper in front of his eyes but placed it in a position where he would be able to view what was happening in front of him while still being able to read the paper. A few minutes after the pretty girl had passed the train arrived at its first stop in Manhattan. The doors opened and Christopher got up and walked toward the open door. Frasier was sitting on that part of the bench which was closest to the open door with his back to it but directly facing Christopher as he walked towards the door. Frasier testified that at the point Christopher was parallel to him within inches of the open door he saw Christopher's right arm coming at him in an underhanded swinging manner and he instinctively raised his right hand in a defensive position. It was then that Frasier saw the blood gushing from his fingers two of which had been nearly severed.

Frasier was momentarily stunned by what had happened. In fact, he testified that he did not realize that he had been stabbed but he did manage to follow Christopher out the door just before it closed. He had realized that the young white man sitting across from him had done him harm but he did know exactly what it was. He did know that he was in pain. Frasier attempted to follow Christopher on the subway platform but lost him in the crowd. He also realized that he was in immediate need of medical attention as he glanced at his profusely bleeding hand and his partially severed fingers. The police were notified and conducted an immediate search of the subway station but Christopher had once again made a successful escape. Frasier received medical attention but the face of Joseph Christopher was forever branded into his memory and he had no trouble identifying him either at the lineup or in court at the trial. Frasier's quick reflexes had saved his life. If he had not had that split second to raise his hand, Christopher's knife would have surely found its way into his heart.

Each day during the trial, I would go to the holding cell behind the courtroom attempting to discuss my strategy with Christopher. Each time I was met with a wry smile and no further acknowledgement of my presence. I did notice that on each of those occasions Christopher had stuffed cotton into his ears. At first, I thought that he did not want to hear the proceedings during the trial. But as time passed, I realized that he was paying attention to the testimony but was showing no emotion. I then suggested to him that the reason he had stuffed cotton into his ears was in a futile attempt to block out the voices which only he heard. When I confronted Christopher with my theory it was the only time I witnessed a change in his demeanor. For a few seconds, he raised his eyebrows and gave me a look of surprise. But just as quickly the brief change of expression returned itself to the more expressionless gaze which had he had featured during most of the time I was with him. There was no question in my mind that he was still conversing with the same voices during the trial that had driven him to his homicidal rages in 1980.

New York City has the largest population of any city in the United States but, in many ways, it can be considered a series of neighborhoods or villages where it is possible to meet someone you recognize but don't really know strictly by coincidence. I'm sure that it has happened to most of us somewhere at some time. What happened during the Christopher trial still has me scratching my head thirty years later. Shortly after the jury had been chosen and testimony had begun, I got a phone call from a lifelong friend from Buffalo named Steve Caruana. Steve was also born and raised in Auburn and his father had been friends with my parents since childhood. He had spent many of his summers in New York City working for his uncles who were well known in the music business in New York. On this occasion, he was attending a conference of a union of Hospital workers of which he was the president. Steve's call had come as a surprise and it took me some time the locate the recently opened Marriott Marquis hotel in mid-Manhattan where he was staying. Joseph Christopher was still big news in Buffalo but New York City had all but forgotten him. Steve had lived in Buffalo for most of his adult life and was surprised to learn that the trial of fellow resident Joe Christopher had just begun. Steve had told me that he had heard a radio interview on one of the Buffalo radio stations between myself and a reporter. The interview was conducted via the telephone and the reporter assured me that everything I said would be off the record. In fact, he was recording every word I uttered without my permission. He then played the entire conversation on the radio and Steve had told me about hearing the interview. There are no words to describe my disgust at the actions of the reporter and I never spoke to another one again about Christopher. Steve's phone call during the trial was coincidence number one.

Coincidence number two happened shortly after number one when Steve and I agreed to meet at the bar of the Marriott Marquis for a drink before going to dinner. When we came down in the elevator from Steve's room, we walked toward the bar where I noticed a group of people sitting at a table near the bar. As we got closer to the table, I noticed one of them who I knew well. It was the foreman of the jury who was probably trying to enjoy himself with friends after the day's testimony at trial. I grabbed Steve and guided him to the revolving door out of the hotel telling him that it was necessary for me to get the hell out of there before the foreman noticed me. The foreman never saw me but I wondered whether the foreman took the judge's instructions seriously enough not discuss anything about the trial with anyone especially among a group of people which potentially had included a large contingent from Buffalo.

The third coincidence which was more startling also happened while I was with Steve. The jury announced its verdict on the evening before Steve was going to leave town. I wanted to blow off a little steam after the rigors of the month-long trial. We decided to go to our favorite restaurant in Little Italy and then walk the entire distance to his hotel near Times Square. When Steve and I were together there was always much to talk about. He was interested in the trial of Joseph Christopher which had caused his home city so much concern in 1980. It was also a great way to walk off a huge dinner. We began our journey north from Mulberry Street in Little Italy and as we approached Washington Square park in the heart of Greenwich Village and appropriately enough just across the street from the NYU Law School, I noticed someone else that I recognized. It was juror number seven.

He recognized me and we met and shook hands. He told me that the deliberations were difficult because most of the jurors believed that Christopher was truly psychotic and not responsible for his actions. But there was not enough evidence of his mental state at the time of the murders to convince them that he was not responsible for his actions as the law required. He went on to tell me that the jury was impressed by my patchwork defense but it simply was not enough to put the defense over the top. I explained Christopher's total lack of cooperation with my attempts to have him psychiatrically evaluated when I took over his case and I pointed to the NYU Law School just across the street as its cause. No Hollywood writer could have scripted our coincidental meeting any better. It was almost too melodramatic to have been believed, but it did happen.

Before I conclude my treatise on Joseph Christopher, I must issue the readers a warning in the form of a disclaimer especially to all of us who watch crime shows on television. To those of us who have watched "The FBI Files" and accept it as gospel, take heed. In 1999, the FBI Files did a show on Joseph Christopher. It was season two, episode eighteen and titled "The .22 Caliber Killer." You can watch it on You Tube although I advise against it at least until you have had a chance to read what follows and then you can make up your own mind as to the quality of the work product. The episode concerned itself with Christopher's actions in Buffalo and seemed to have been fairly accurate in its portrayal of Christopher's reign of terror there. The research necessary to present a more comprehensive picture of the facts seems to have stopped with the interviews with law enforcement personnel in Buffalo. The FBI Files announced that Christopher was convicted and sentenced to sixty-five years to life for the murders in Buffalo some sixteen or seventeen years after those convictions had been overturned by the appellate courts. The Files then went on to characterize army nurse Anderson as a female and even had a female actress portray him for dramatic effect. The actress was certainly prettier than the real nurse Anderson. The Files then concluded the episode by announcing that Christopher had never been tried for the murders in New York City even though the trial had taken place fourteen years earlier. They also mischaracterized the murder of Luis Rodriguez as a robbery.

There exists the reality of the limitations of a thirty-minute program in which to inform the viewers of all the relevant facts but to mislead the same viewers with a casual untruth at the very end of the program really calls into question the integrity of the entire program. The FBI itself probably had nothing to do with the writing but it did lend its name to the program with the purpose of impressing the viewing public with the program's infallibility. I might be exaggerating the effect of such malfeasance, but crime programs have become very popular and undoubtedly influence all of us who watch them. All of us who one day may sit in judgment of a Joseph Christopher or any other individual charged with a crime.

The trial ended with Dr. Joseph's testimony. The defense was then called upon to give its summation. The purpose of a summation is to give both the prosecution and defense one last opportunity to convince the jury of their point of view of the evidence. I started by repeating the phase I had first mentioned in my opening statement which is the title of this Chapter.

"Joseph Christopher is a very sick individual. His view of reality is not at all like ours."

I argued that Christopher should be placed in an institution where he could be studied and not confined to prison where his psychosis would only fester and grow worse. In that way, we could learn more about the psychology of such rare individuals who seem to grow normally as children yet develop into dangerous psychopaths as adults. I admonished the jury that society was going to produce more serial killers like Christopher and that they had a golden opportunity to add to the body of knowledge which might identify those dangerous individuals before they had a chance to act upon their twisted beliefs. I believe that history has given validity to my words but it didn't take a genius to figure that out.

Jim Fogel then gave his summation on behalf of the People of the State of New York. Fogel called Christopher a "virulent racist" bent on the destruction of anyone one with dark skin. He accentuated the heinousness and wantonness of Christopher's crimes and that he had to be removed from society in order to protect society from his homicidal rages. Christopher had shown evidence of rational thought of self-preservation in his ability to escape detection for such an extended period before he was captured. Furthermore, the nature of his crimes evinced calculated thought in the manner they were carried out.

Upon the conclusion of our summations, Justice John A.K. Bradley charged the jury as to the law they should apply to their findings of fact including the law defining not guilty by reason of insanity. They deliberated for about two and one-half days but rejected the insanity defense and found Christopher guilty of Murder in the Second Degree for the murder of Luis Rodriguez and Attempted Murder in the Second Degree for the assault on Ivan Frasier. According to juror seven, it was a difficult deliberation as was evidenced by the amount of time it took to reach a decision. A few weeks later, Justice Bradley handed down the maximum sentence of twenty-five years to life for Murder in the Second degree and eight and one-third to twenty-five years for Attempted Murder in the Second Degree. The sentences were to run consecutively to each other which made the total thirty-three and one third years to life.

Christopher eventually went back to Buffalo to be retried for the 1980 murders. I am not sure what happened there but I did receive a telephone call from his mother about a year later. She told me that her son wanted her to thank me for my efforts on his behalf and that he was cooperating with his lawyers in Buffalo. I believe that he may have been convicted of the lesser charge of Manslaughter after psychiatric testimony was allowed into evidence in the Buffalo court. Joseph Christopher died of a rare form of male breast cancer in prison not far from where he grew up on March 1, 1993. He was thirty-eight years old and was still serving the sentence in my case. He would have been eligible for parole in 2014.

VII. THE MADNESS OF TWO

During most of the twentieth century, the Soviet Union was a place of great concern for the United States. The Cold War was aptly named as a description of the relationship between the two countries. The fear of nuclear war led to anger and distrust which developed into a bitter rivalry for many generations until Communism collapsed in 1989. While persecution and discrimination of minorities existed in both countries, the Soviet Union was a brutal dictatorship for most of those years which sanctioned the repression of many groups including religious minorities. Religious worship was outlawed and punished. Jews were particularly identified, isolated and punished for practicing their religion. Such was the situation of the Kagan family of Belarus, Russia. The Kagans consisted of the mother, father, a son and daughter and two grandparents. They attempted to practice their religion of Judaism but found that an impossible task in Belarus. In the early1980s, they applied for and were granted asylum in the United States largely through the efforts of the Jewish relief organizations in New York City.

The Kagan family arrived in New York around 1981 but did not originally include the grandparents. Once the mother, father and children were situated, the grandparents followed. They settled on the lower eastside following the tradition of their ancestors who had arrived a century earlier. It was difficult for the family to find work and were mostly supported by the Jewish organizations which had sponsored them. The family of four lived in one apartment while the grandparents lived separately. The family was very well educated in the Soviet Union and the mother, Rosa, was a practicing dentist in Belarus.

Daughter Yulia was in her late teens when she arrived and was intelligent and educated with the ability to speak English as was her mother. Unable to find meaningful employment in New York, Rosa began experiencing psychological problems. She started hearing voices and grew increasingly paranoid. Rosa had much difficulty adjusting to life in the United States and particularly to the diversity of cultures that existed in New York City. As Rosa's mental illness became more pronounced, the fabric of the family began to fray and tear apart.

Rosa and Yulia grew very close emotionally and spiritually while the son and father became increasingly isolated from the women. At a certain point, the father found it impossible to live with his wife and daughter and he left them taking his son with him. The women were placed in an apartment in the Washington Heights section of upper Manhattan while the father and son remained on the lower eastside near the grandparents. There was no attempt to treat Rosa's illness and, as you might expect, her paranoid thoughts became a psychosis. Yulia did not suffer from the same paranoid delusions as Rosa but she was devoted to her mother and soon developed similar symptoms. Their residence in the apartment in Washington Heights became a scene of such great physical destruction and emotional chaos that it resulted in their eviction. Having no other place to live, they moved in with the grandparents which became a very fateful and tragic decision.

While in their apartment in Washington Heights, Rosa and Yulia's delusions led them to believe that people were looking at them through the cracks in the bathroom walls. People existed in their kitchen sink drains and were trying to make their way out to do them harm or to simply spy on them. These same apparitions were spying on them through the apartment windows and overhead light fixtures. They attempted to protect themselves by taking hammer and chisel to the bathroom walls, painting over all the windows, destroying the sinks and toilet and ripping out the light fixtures. They annoyed neighbors by asking to use their toilets after they had destroyed their own. All of this was chronicled in a diary which was written in English by Yulia who was more proficient in the language than her mother. They existed in constant darkness and only ventured outside the building to obtain food. The landlord was receiving the rent directly from public assistance but once he viewed the apartment, they were quickly evicted and the tragic move was made to the apartment of Rosa's parents.

The vitriol resulting from Rosa's paranoia was directed at her father. Rosa hated her father for no rational reason. She suffered from paranoid delusions one of which was the belief that her father had purchased her at an outdoor market when she was a baby and was not her natural father. This delusional belief gradually morphed into an irrational hate. The relationship was at best tenuous when Rosa lived with her parents but they relied on both Rosa and Yulia for assistance in their daily activities. The grandparents did not like living in the United States, and were not happy with their lives in New York or the living arrangements on the lower eastside. Yulia did not suffer from the same degree of paranoia as her mother but she did suffer from the same irrational beliefs as her mother. Yulia robotically obeyed Rosa's every wish without thought. One day all the sadness, hate and delusional thinking exploded into the horrific deaths of the grandparents.

Rosa stabbed and strangled her father, kicked in his ribs, fractured his skull and knocked out several of his teeth. The grandmother was treated more gently but she too was dispatched but only by strangulation. Her body was found with a white bath towel around her neck. The towel had a green stripe length wise down the middle which was embroidered with the name of Grossinger's, the once famous but now defunct hotel located in the Catskill mountains about one hundred miles north of New York City. Grossinger's was a popular destination which catered mostly to the Jewish people of New York who wanted to get away from the hustle and bustle of the City. Many famous comedians had cut their teeth on the stage at Grossinger's. That section of the Catskills was so popular with the Jewish community that it was called the "borscht belt" or the "Jewish Alps." How one of Mr. Grossinger's bath towels found its way around the neck of an elderly homicide victim was another story.

The bodies were placed on the floor lengthwise, head to foot and wrapped in white linen. Candles were lit and placed lengthwise on each side of the bodies, head to foot. Rosa and Yulia were determined to prepare the bodies for burial according to Judaic tradition, but since they were never allowed to practice their religion in the Soviet Union, they were unsure if they had done the right thing. Yulia decided to call her father to ask if he had any idea if they had proceeded in the correct manner. The father quickly realized that something was very wrong. He rushed over to the scene of the impromptu funeral and immediately notified the police.

When the police arrived, they saw the bodies wrapped in linen and the position of the candles and thought that this was a scene of a ritual sacrifice. The New York tabloids screamed "Occult Killings on Lower Eastside." All Rosa and Yulia were trying to do was to conduct a Jewish ceremony but the scene did look rather bizarre and the tabloids saw an opportunity to sensationalize the killings more than they were in themselves. Both Rosa and Yulia made full confessions and the bizarre content of the statements would give any reader cause to doubt the sanity of both women. Rosa recounted the story of her purchase as a baby at the market in the Soviet Union. This gave her more than enough reason to kill her father who was, undoubtedly, not her real father. She exhibited little remorse and seemed confused as to why the police doubted her reasoning. Yulia was not as emotional in her statement but agreed with her mother as to the reason her grandfather deserved to die. Both Rosa and Yulia were indicted on two counts of Murder in the Second Degree and I undertook the task of representing Yulia.

The women faced a minimum of fifteen years to life and a maximum of twenty-five years to life for each Murder count in the indictment. The total jail time each faced was fifty years to life, if convicted. The first time I met Yulia was in the holding pens next to the courtroom about a week after she and her mother had been arrested. Rosa was in the pen next to her daughter which was separated by a wall and had a different entrance. Since both pens were on the same side, the women could not see each other, but were able to converse. The women had been in custody for about a week, but received no treatment for their rather obvious mental illnesses. Yulia was calm but very confused and had the look of a deer in the headlights. Rosa, on the other hand, was wild-eyed and uncontrollable. Still suffering from her homicidal rage, she had to be placed in a special jacket something akin to a strait jacket to prevent her from doing harm to herself when she made her initial court appearance. Yulia, more demure than her mother, needed no restraint at all. When I first met Yulia, it was plainly obvious that she was still delusional. As a result, there existed the possibility that she was also not competent to understand the proceedings against her. She knew that she had been arrested but certainly did not understand what was going on in the courtroom. She was unwittingly cooperating in her defense but the irrational answers to my questions would assuredly fit the profile of one who was not able to cooperate in her defense at all. I wanted Yulia as close to her mental state as possible as when the murders had occurred.

I quickly determined that valuable time would be wasted if I had asked the judge to have her examined by court psychiatrists on the issue of competency. The final copy of the report would usually take two to three months to complete. Sometimes it took longer. During that time, Yulia would have been given some type of psychotropic medication to ease her symptoms and force fed the answers to questions revolving around the issue of competency. The questions usually consisted of knowing the function of her lawyer, the prosecutor and the judge. I did not want any part of such court intrigue so I did not ask the judge to order what is categorized an Article 730 examination by the Criminal Procedure Law. The case was in front of the late Hon. Harold Rothwax who was a former attorney for the Legal Aid Society before being elevated to the bench. He was a terror in the courtroom to both defense and prosecution. If a defendant went to trial in front of Judge Rothwax and lost, said defendant could kiss a certain part of his anatomy goodbye forever. But Judge Rothwax was also an adjunct professor at Columbia Law School with a scholastic bent. It was urgently necessary that I convince him that Yulia knew what was going on so he would sign an order having her examined by a psychiatrist of my choosing as to criminal responsibility rather than competency. If he thought that I was trying to pull the wool over his eyes, which I was, he would have ignored my request and ordered the dreaded Article 730 examination. I somehow managed to convince a very tough and skeptical jurist and he signed my order. It was my piece de resistance of bullshit because everyone in the courtroom knew that Yulia was lost and confused.

Everyone remembers the case of the State of California versus O.J. Simpson. Much of the reason for the success of his defense besides having an incredibly obtuse jury, was the fact that his attorneys were on the case almost immediately after Simpson was arrested. The famous and now infamous forensic blood analyst Henry Lee was on the red eye from New York to Los Angeles the very evening of Simpson's arrest. He developed much of the evidence the defense used countering the sloppy investigation done by the police. Lee was breathing down their necks as they investigated the crime scene and may have even suggested "if the glove don't fit, you must acquit" tactic used by Johnnie Cochran knowing that a glove soaked in blood will shrink. I had my own experience with Henry Lee in another homicide case four years earlier. I was breathing down the necks of the Department of Corrections and the court attempting to have Yulia examined before they had a chance to get their hands on her. The day of her first appearance in Judge Rothwax's court I went to the holding pens just after her appearance and interviewed her for approximately five hours. She related a story which stretched the boundaries of sanity to their limit. Basically, she repeated the delusion of her mother that of the Rosa's purchase as a baby at the open-air market. I asked her why she believed her mother's story when her mother had never mentioned it when they were a family in Belarus. Yulia answered her mother must be correct in her delusion because Rosa had convinced her that it was true and that Yulia's grandfather bore no resemblance to her mother. I asked Yulia if Rosa looked like her grandmother and if Rosa had ever confronted her grandmother about her allegations. Yulia gave me a blank stare and never answered the question.

During most of the five-hour interview, my direct questions concerning her mother's behavior leading up to the murders were met with silence and indignation. Any suggestion that her mother was not in her right mind was usually met with another question as to why I would ask the question in the first place. Yulia was totally under the influence of her psychotic mother. I had taken the precaution of interviewing her in another area of the holding pens away from her mother. In fact, her mother was on a separate floor but it was as if Rosa were sitting next to her daughter whispering in her ear. Yulia would volunteer accounts of the heroic deeds of her mother. On one occasion, she told me the story of how her mother had saved her grandmother's life. The grandmother had developed an infection in her arm and the doctors wanted to amputate. In some way, Rosa intervened and saved her mother's arm thereby saving her life. I was tempted to ask Yulia why Rosa had bothered to save her mother in the first place. But this was not an occasion for sarcasm and I don't think Yulia would not have understood my foolish attempt at humor anyway. Yulia could not give me any reason as to how Rosa had saved her grandmother's life, but she was absolutely convinced that it was true.

At the end of the five hours I concluded with the question that was most paramount in my mind. If Yulia's grandfather was the source of her mother's homicidal fury, why then was her grandmother murdered? Yulia and Rosa were both so psychotic that I didn't think that they worried about leaving witnesses.

Yulia told me that Rosa thought that her mother would get lonely without her husband so the most humane thing to do was to send her grandmother to the same place as her grandfather so they could be together forever. Very reminiscent of the famous play and movie "Arsenic and Old Lace" where the loveable spinster sisters would poison their house guests because they thought it would be the most humane gesture to relieve their guests of their loneliness. I concluded that, from the condition of the bodies, Rosa had killed her father but it must have taken both using such a crude device as a bath towel to choke the life out of the grandmother. She must have suffered greatly before she took her last breath.

I had taken copious notes during the interview that only a psychiatrist could decipher. I engaged the services of a psychiatrist and showed him my notes. When dealing with psychiatrists it has been my experience that they are prone to change their opinions from one day to the next. The psychiatrist who I had engaged told me that he thought it was a case of shared paranoid delusion or in medical terms a Folie a Deux. Roughly translated it means "the Madness of Two" thus giving this Chapter its title. Folie a Deux is a very rare mental illness and even more difficult to prove. You must establish that two individuals somehow shared the same delusional thoughts. Mental illness is not a virus which can be transmitted from one person to another but thoughts which can be easily transmitted through speech. How do you determine if one person is simply parroting the thoughts of another without suffering from a mental illness and then expressing those thoughts as a matter of social discourse? It is on one hand easy to fake a mental illness using the symptoms of the disease but it would take a very sophisticated malingerer to pull it off. Schizophrenia, bi-polar disorders and dementia are the usual choices of the practiced malingerer. I hoped that my psychiatrist would not change his opinion after mulling it over. Unfortunately, I do not remember the psychiatrist's name but he never changed his diagnosis and it was reinforced when he interviewed Yulia herself.

The interview took place a few weeks after Yulia had been arrested. By that time, Yulia had been plied with drugs to stabilize her but it was still close enough to the act for my psychiatrist to get a real flavor of her mental state when the murders were committed. My psychiatrist relied heavily on my impressions of Yulia during the five-hour interview. It took a few months for him to formulate his opinion. At one point, I thought he was questioning his initial diagnosis. He called upon me more than once to repeat the substance of the five-hour interview and my description of the conversations I had with Yulia since the first interview. He probably was unsure because I could sense the doubt in his voice when I talked to him. He finalized his diagnosis of shared paranoid delusion in a report which I served upon the District Attorney and with Judge Rothwax several months after Yulia had been taken into custody.

It took the District Attorney's psychiatrist four or five more months to interview, formulate an opinion and issue a written report on Yulia. I thought the defense was going to have a difficult time establishing Yulia's defense. After all this was a double homicide involving both matricide and patricide. Any conviction would surely have resulted in two life sentences for both women. Yulia was probably young enough to get paroled in her lifetime, but Rosa would certainly have spent the remainder of her years behind bars. Judge Rothwax was fully capable of handing down such a sentence but he was also intrigued by the diagnosis of shared paranoid delusion. I had learned from one of his students at Columbia Law School that he was eagerly anticipating presiding over a trial which would attract the attention of the legal community. Judge Rothwax had invited his students to view the proceedings once the trial started. It would have been even more interesting to students and legal scholars because I had informed Judge Rothwax that I was going to invoke the trial tactic of bifurcation. In a bifurcated trial, there would be two separate trials. One to determine actual guilt and the other to determine criminal responsibility. There are many logistical problems with such a maneuver but it would relieve the defense of having to admit to the jury that Yulia had, in fact, committed the murders. Once the jury had determined guilt the trial could then move on the criminal responsibility stage and the defense of not guilty by reason of insanity. If she was found not guilty in the first instance, there would be no need to determine criminal responsibility.

It would be entirely at the discretion of Judge Rothwax to permit such a rare procedure but it is not unknown in the law. This was the perfect case for a bifurcation. The defendants were both scholarly, well educated women with no criminal history and not at all acquainted with the customs and laws of the United States which would have given rise to a greater opportunity for malingering. I believed that Judge Rothwax would have permitted it but a trial, bifurcated or otherwise, was short circuited when the psychiatrist engaged by the

District Attorney wholeheartedly agreed that this was indeed a classic case of Folie a Deux. Both women would be allowed to plead not guilty by reason of insanity and placed in the custody of the commissioner of Mental Hygiene for an indefinite period of time until such a time when they were cured of their illness and no longer constituted a threat to the community. It took about a year for the case to reach its conclusion. During its pendency, it was agreed between the parties and the judge that Yulia have as little contact with her mother as possible. Judge Rothwax ordered that the women be sent to different facilities for treatment and would be permitted to communicate by letter only. The day Yulia was ordered to a mental health facility, she expressed remorse and understood that she was very sick when she committed the murders and that her confinement in a psychiatric hospital could last a lifetime.

When Yulia made her final appearance in Judge Rothwax's courtroom, I fully expected never to see her again. I thought she would be confined for at least a couple of decades before she would be let back into the community, if at all. Never say never. I found myself representing Yulia again in Judge Rothwax's courtroom about three years after she had been sent to the state hospital. I received a call from the judge's courtroom attorney who informed me that Yulia's case was back on the calendar. During the three years she had been hospitalized at the Kirby Forensic Center located on Ward's Island in the East River not far from the Triboro Bridge. She had progressed rapidly in her treatment and was being allowed the privilege of both escorted and unescorted furloughs around the hospital campus. These furloughs would become more relaxed dependent upon Yulia's positive response to treatment. She had responded so well to her treatment that she was about to be rewarded with escorted furloughs off Ward's Island and into Manhattan itself when she ran afoul of the attorney for the damned. Then her situation changed drastically.

State psychiatric hospitals have a cadre of attorneys who are assigned to the hospitals to protect the rights of the patients. This particular attorney whom I have labeled the "attorney for the damned" had published a book of the same title describing his experiences in psychiatric hospitals. The unfortunate residents of these institutions were the damned but to consider the author to be an actual attorney for them would take a quantum leap. Yulia had been proceeding very nicely through the various stages of release leading up to final release. The reports of attending psychiatrists were effusive in their admiration of Yulia's progress. The attorney for the damned evidently thought otherwise and for some inexplicable reason, he decided to have her evaluated by an independent psychiatrist. The psychiatrist he chose was Dr. Train not John Train who had a great reputation in the field of forensic psychiatry, but his brother Arthur who did not have such a reputation. Arthur Train took a much more moralistic approach toward his practice of psychiatry and issued a report indicating that Yulia should never be released to the outside world and basically should rot in hell for what she did. I have never read a psychiatric report before or since with such a good versus evil approach to psychoanalysis. There were so many cross references to religion and philosophy that the report could have easily gain the approval of the Catholic Church for publication. This report had to be dealt with before Yulia could progress in her treatment.

Yulia was smart and it did not take her long to figure out that the attorney for the damned was no damned good. She wrote a letter to Judge Rothwax outlining her situation and requested relief. Specifically, she requested that I represent her again in his courtroom. This request precipitated the phone call from Judge Rothwax. I agreed to represent Yulia who was challenging Dr. Arthur Train's report. About two weeks later the case was sent to Justice Allen Murray Meyer for a hearing as to Yulia's status in the hospital. It was said that if all the cases were sent to Judge Meyer, Judge Rothwax and a couple of other notable jurists, there would no jury trials. All the defendants would quickly realize their predicament and plead guilty to cut their losses. Present were three treating psychiatrists from Kirby Forensic, Dr. Arthur Train, the attorney for the damned and his supervisor, Yulia, myself and an assistant attorney general representing the Commissioner of Mental Hygiene.

Prior to the start of the proceedings, I approached the attorney for the damned and told him that I would be damned if I could think of a reason why he would ask for an independent evaluation especially since Yulia's progress reports were so glowing? Perhaps I'm shooting myself in the foot, but I have found that lawyers who are published take on an aura of smugness and condescension. Their words take on an air of infallibility and cannot be challenged. This was certainly the attitude of the attorney for the damned who responded that I didn't know what I was doing. I repeated to him the substance of an earlier conversation with his supervisor in which I had indicated that he had undone in a few short weeks what it had taken me over a year to accomplish.

Then I called him an idiot for engaging the services of the wrong Dr. Train and that even a poor soul like Yulia Kagan could see how incompetent he was. The final insult was that I accused him of stealing the title of his book from a book written by Clarence Darrow famous for the Scopes trial on evolution in the 1920s but not published until the late 1950s long after Darrow's death. The response was a look to kill. Dr. Train's objectivity was easy fodder for cross examination and Judge Meyer issued an opinion restoring Yulia's status. When I looked around the courtroom the attorney for the damned had disappeared and I never saw him again.

The Kagans spent less than five years in the psychiatric hospitals before they were discharged into the community. This was truly an incredible outcome for any defendant who faced the possibility of a lifetime of incarceration for a double homicide. Yulia and Rosa Kagan were perfect candidates for such a resolution to their cases. When it comes to psychiatric disabilities, the law is an ass. The madness of most individuals in today's world is multi-layered. These individuals could be suffering from a Folie a Deux but given the complexities of life in the 20th century it is difficult to peel away the layers of learned behavior to get to the actual source of the psychosis. The standard for an insanity defense is the McNaughton Rule which is very difficult to establish. The Kagans had come from a far less complicated culture more akin to life in the 19th century when the Rule was promulgated and not influenced by the clash of cultures that exist in New York City. They were naïve subjects with fewer layers to peel away and much easier to diagnose. A textbook case of the madness of two.

A few months after Yulia had been released from the hospital I received a phone call from Rosa Kagan. Yulia wanted an appointment with me to discuss her options. I agreed and a week later Yulia and I met in my office. It was the first time I had seen her since the fiasco with the lawyer for the damned. She certainly looked much better than when I had last seen her. She was calm, engaging and well groomed. She and her mother had just been moved from a shelter to their own apartments in the Bronx. They were not living together but visited very often. I questioned the advisability of the consistent contact with her mother but she told me that her mother was cured and that she was a much stronger person. She indicated that she had learned much about her illness during her confinement and she was confident that there would little

71

chance of another Folie a Deux. The conversation had more to do with her intention to have a romantic relationship with me than her living status. I realized this almost immediately and proceeded cautiously. She was cured but did not understand that my actions in defending her were purely professional.

I let her do most of the talking and did not respond to her romantic overtures. Given her fragile emotional state, I thought the better part of valor was to keep my mouth shut. After about an hour, Yulia abandoned her romantic dreams and left the office. I never saw her again. I suppose therapists would classify her desires as transference where the patients misinterpret the role of the therapists as a love interest in them. A few days later I did receive a call from Rosa inquiring as to the cost of my advice. I told her it was not necessary to compensate me. She thanked me but I detected the guilt and remorse in her voice that her mental illness had destroyed the life of her young daughter. I told her that I hoped that she and Yulia could successfully carry on with their lives and wished them well. I never heard from them again.

VIII. The Troll And
The Five Hundred Pound Woman

Once upon a time in the early 1980s, there existed a troll like individual named Lou Miranda. Lou lived in the basement of his brownstone apartment building on the eastside of Manhattan. True to his troll instincts, Lou chose to live in his subterranean digs as far away from human contact as possible. Humans were hated and reviled for most were of normal height and bore non-troll like faces. They were good only for loaning Lou money so he could speculate in the volatile real estate market in New York. Lou was really a human being but he possessed the magical qualities of a troll for everywhere Lou went for mortgage money, he was never refused. But one sad day he approached a fellow Italian named Thomas Vigliarolo for a mortgage loan. Lou invoked his magical troll powers but was refused. Thomas Vigliarolo was in the business of mortgage lending and had lots of money so Lou could not understand why he was rejected. It must have been that the mortgage lender was immune to his troll-like powers and bitter resentment grew in the heart of Lou the troll. It is never wise to mess with a troll or a sixty-five-year-old human who could be easily mistaken for a troll.

The bitter resentment grew into an all-consuming hate and about three years after he had been rejected, Lou Miranda decided that it was time to act. He decided upon a melodrama featuring seven players including himself. Miranda would be the director, producer and writer for the written word always had room enough for the creative thought of a giant intellect. Miranda had concluded that Vigliarolo owed him the principal of the requested loan, the profit he would have made had he been able to invest the loan plus three years of interest compounded. The plan to recoup his lost profits was set in motion when he approached a friend named Marie Talag, a Filipina national, who had emigrated from her country after getting involved in some shady business there. The plan was to kidnap Vigliarolo and hold him for a ransom which, not coincidentally, matched the exact amount Miranda figured was owed to him. Vigliarolo would be lured to Talag's apartment in Queens with the promise of sexual favors bestowed upon him by three beautiful young women named Donna Hylton, Rita Peters and Theresa Holland. The three women who would later be referred to as the "Pointer Sisters" after the popular singing group of that era, worked at the Milford Plaza Hotel with Talag. The Milford Plaza was located in the heart of the theatre district and catered to all kinds of visitors including visiting firemen as we euphemistically put it. The young women were all beautiful and had an interest in modeling and acting but I suspected that, in furtherance of their ambitions, they acted as courtesans for the visiting firemen at the hotel. Their coordinator was Marie Talag who, herself, was suspected of occasional interludes of gay, sadomasochistic sex at the hotel.

Miranda aka Lou the troll approached Vigliarolo again about a mortgage loan but Vigliarolo lived on Long Island and it was vital that he be lured to the apartment in Queens. Miranda tried to sweeten the deal by offering a romantic rendezvous with the young women at Talag's apartment. He couldn't possibly have offered Talag herself for Talag's looks would have stopped a charging rhinoceros in its tracks and the whole scheme would have collapsed. The other players in this drama were Woody Pace and his wife Selma Price who had an apartment in Harlem. Pace was a convicted felon who had spent much of his youth in state prison while Price passed every waking moment gorging herself with food attempting to cure her depression over his continuous absence until she blew up to over five hundred pounds. Woody had a face only Selma could love but I doubt whether the actual marriage was consummated. No one could get into the same bed with Price or be so acrobatic as to fulfill their husbandly obligations to her. The scene was set and everyone had their part. With Lou the troll in command of this ship of fools, what could possibly go wrong?

The plan was to lure Vigliarolo to the apartment introduce him to the young women, ply him with alcohol then have Woody Pace come into the apartment tie and gag Vigliarolo and throw him into the back of a van rented specially for that purpose. The gang would then drive their captive to the apartment of Pace and Price in Harlem where Miranda would be waiting. All this was accomplished without incident. The captivity began and ended in that apartment. A living hell where Tom Vigliarolo would met his fate stuffed in a steamer trunk after enduring unspeakable torture for several days. All the players were eventually arrested and I took up the representation of Donna Hylton the most beautiful of the three women.

The story began when Talag approached Hylton, Peters and Holland and induced them to get involved with the promise of a career in modeling if they successfully played their part in the scheme. When you have stars in your eyes like these three women, you lose touch with reality and agree to almost anything that would make your dreams come true. After meeting their leader, Lou the troll, you would think that they had more sense than to believe anything he said. But that was not the case and they soon were in so deep that there was no turning back. Hylton, my client, was assigned the task of renting the van which carried Vigliarolo to the apartment in Harlem. She went to a rental agency on west ninety-six street where she was a steady customer. This agency accepted cash which made it much more convenient for Hylton to rent the van. The van would later become the single most significant factor in the breakup of the scheme and the arrest of everyone involved.

In Price's apartment, Vigliarolo was beaten, bound and gagged, tortured, starved and finally suffocated. The torture consisted of ramming a lead pipe into the anus of Tom Vigliarolo and was mainly inflicted by Pace, Miranda and Talag who seemed to have an expertise in sadomasochistic behavior. The beatings and torture took place in a bedroom next to the bedroom occupied by the whale like body of Selma Price who rarely moved off her bed. Selma Price was a stunningly obese woman. She could best be described as five feet tall and five feet wide. One would have to find some way to navigate around Price's huge body to get to the front door of the apartment. It seemed that Price's only role in this tragic melodrama was to act as a natural obstacle to any attempt by Vigliarolo to escape his confinement. Hylton, Peters and Holland were assigned watch duty on a rotating basis.

The scheme which was designed to find the pot of gold at the end of the rainbow was hardly well planned. With Lou Miranda making all the decisions, you could understand why. The gang made more mistakes than you could count on your fingers and toes. They made virtually no attempt to cover their tracks. The van was driven several times to rendezvous points in Long island where Vigliarolo lived where it could easily be seen. The van, itself, acted as a portable office where ransom notes were typed and recorded. The gang never changed the license plates and was a shade of white which was as bright as a full moon. At one point, Hylton made a delivery of a ransom note to Vigliarolo's office building. She used the same white van with the same license plates and made no effort to disguise her appearance. One of the ransom notes that was recorded for use over a telephone was discovered in the back of the van with Rita Peter's fingerprints. They made no attempt to reassure the family that Vigliarolo was being treated well or was even alive.

During his confinement, Tom Vigliarolo suffered immensely. What little care afforded him was provided by Hylton and Holland. Peters was not around very much but when she was there it seemed to be when Vigliarolo was being tortured. She had a hard edge to her personality and was the least sympathetic of the group, aka the Pointer Sisters. Theresa Holland was not the brightest star in the sky. Even Lou the troll realized this and assigned her only tasks which required very little thought. Unfortunately, one of these tasks was to assist in holding Vigliarolo down as he was being tortured. Holland was the most gullible and compliant of the Pointer Sisters. Throughout all of this, she harbored the misguided belief that what she was doing would eventually lead to a career in modeling and fame and fortune on the runway.

The most sympathetic of the three was Donna Hylton. Beautiful, intelligent, and manipulative, she could have had any man she wanted. The trial judge, Justice Edwin Torres, once proclaimed that she was one of the most beautiful woman to have ever entered his courtroom. She was the most likely of the three to have a career in modeling but, like many other of my female clients, she suffered from the "bad boy" syndrome. She was hopelessly attracted to the wrong kind of man and resultant lifestyle. Giving birth to a daughter out of wedlock only exacerbated her situation. She seemed to have had a solid foundation growing up but her good looks always seemed to get in the way.

Hylton was the most caring and attentive to Vigliarolo's plight often disobeying Miranda's orders by providing him with more food and water than instructed. Hylton had realized early on what she had gotten herself into but also realized that it was too late to back out. She was remorseful and knew that Vigliarolo was dying but was too frightened to help as all three women had been threatened by Pace and Miranda that they had better keep their mouths shut or they would end up like their captive. Hylton had rented the van with a valid driver's license but incorrect address. Since she used cash for the rental, there was no easy way to trace Hylton when it became overdue. But she was known to the manager and had a history with the company, so no alarm was raised. On one fateful occasion after the van was overdue, the manager was driving his own car somewhere on the west side of Manhattan when he noticed Hylton driving the white van. He pointed his finger at her in the direction of the rental office as if to indicate that she should drive the van back to the office. Hylton acknowledged his gesture with a smile but continued on her way. The manager would later testify for the prosecution as to this seemingly insignificant incident as evidence that Hylton had possession of the van during the time of the kidnapping. If it were another woman not as beautiful as Donna Hylton, I'm sure he would have never remembered the incident. What did I say about her good looks always getting in the way?

The kidnapping incident happened sometime in the early part of June 1985. Within a week or so, the Long Island cops were hot on the trail of the white van having received a description of it from a security guard at Vigliarolo's office building. Evidently, Hylton had parked the van in front of the building when she delivered the envelope containing the ransom note. Master criminals this band of brigands. The arrest of Donna Hylton took place a short time later when she attempted to return the van to the rental agency. When she arrived, she was told to drive the van directly to the garage located below street level. This was an unusual request because that is usually the job of the parking attendants. This raised no suspicion in Hylton's mind until she found herself surrounded by a bevy of law enforcement personnel when she entered the garage. The law enforcement personnel included several officers from the New York City and Long Island police forces and the FBI. The arrest took place out of the view of the general public so as to preserve the privacy of the arrest. Hylton quickly gave up all the players in the scheme after being reminded by one of the Long Island cops that if she did not her "tits would be hanging down past her waist" by the time she got out of jail.

Donna Hylton proceeded to take the police on an odyssey starting with the horrific scene at Selma Price's apartment. When the police broke in the door, they immediately came upon her gargantuan figure lying in her bed. Price needed considerable assistance in lifting her five-hundred-pound frame or even shifting from side to side. A large bedpan was strategically located on the floor of the bedroom near the bed. I never asked Donna whether she or the other women were required to empty the bedpan as part of their quest for fame and fortune, but it really seemed as if Price needed a lot of help in carrying out the most elementary of movements. Hylton directed the police to the back bedroom but first they had to traverse the human obstacle course that was Selma Price. When they entered the back bedroom, they encountered some of the tools of the medieval torture with which Tom Vigliarolo had to endure before death ended his suffering. There were pliers, a vise like grip, electric wires and most significantly an iron bar which the autopsy revealed was more than likely the instrument used to do the greatest damage to Vigliarolo's physical well-being.

At the foot of the bed there was a large steamer trunk which Hylton pointed to as Vigliarolo's make shift coffin. When the trunk was opened the room became enveloped by the stench of Vigliarolo's rotting carcass and from the state of the body, the stench had been there for quite some time. The body was folded like a paper doll, the skin was beginning to rot and several of the large bones were broken to fit the body into the trunk and close it. When I saw the autopsy report, I wondered whether the bones had been broken pre- or posthumously or both. Vigliarolo had been mercifully dead for a few days before his body was discovered. What an ignominious end to anyone's life. What an evil troll was this Louis of Miranda.

Price was arrested on the spot and transported to central booking. I imagine it required a very large police vehicle to accomplish this feat and several officers to get her off the bed. Hylton continued her odyssey with the police pointing out the location of the rest of her accomplices and within twenty-four hours all of them were in custody. They were not hard to find and made no attempt to avoid capture. Hylton also told the police about a Filipino accountant who was a friend of Marie Talag whose function was to launder the ransom money. He was interrogated but never charged. During her odyssey with the police, Hylton confessed her role and the role of her accomplices. The police basically had the case wrapped up within one day after her arrest. All that was left was tying up loose ends and searching for witnesses who would bolster their case.

Shortly after her arraignment, Hylton stood for a lineup for the purpose of having the security guard at Vigliarolo's office building identify her as the person who had delivered the ransom note using the bright, white van. The witness walked into the darkened room where a detective and I were standing. There was a one-way mirror directly in front of us which permitted a view of Hylton and five fill-ins who were especially chosen to resemble Hylton. Most of the fill-ins were of similar height, weight and age as Hylton but none were as beautiful. The witness, who seemed very nervous, looked briefly at the array of women and quickly announced that he did not recognize anyone. When asked by the detective if he was sure that he did not recognize anyone, he said he was and failed to look at the lineup again as was requested by the detective. The witness then hurried out of the room never to be seen again. This was significant because later when I was trying to negotiate a favorable guilty plea for my client the District Attorney refused citing the failure of the witness to identify Hylton. The reason he gave was that Hylton had changed her hairdo before the lineup when warned not to. I countered by pointing out that neither of us knew the nature of her hair styling when the ransom note had been delivered. I then told him that it was my impression that the witness did not want anything to do with the case and that he would not have identified her even if she were wearing a sign around her neck bearing the words "I did it" in large block letters. I finally reminded him that anyone seeing her face would have a hard time forgetting it. To no avail. Donna Hylton would face the full wrath of the criminal justice system.

The court proceedings began in November 1985 with pre-trial hearings before the Hon. Edwin Torres. At the beginning of the case, each defense attorney is required to file a written motion challenging the admission of evidence seized by the police. These basic motions are usually concerned with the suppression of evidence due to improper police conduct. The judge reads the written motions and then orders a hearing with sworn testimony testing the validity of the police conduct. I, of course, attempted to have Hylton's confession to the police suppressed in evidence as did the other attorneys whose clients made similar statements. Various other forms of relief challenging police conduct are also requested and this culminates into full blown hearing after which the judge renders a decision either granting or denying the attorney's request to suppress the evidence. In front of Judge Torres, there was a ninety-nine-point-nine percent probability that the defense's requests will be denied.

Then began the drama within the drama between the seven defense attorneys and Judge Torres. The pre-trial hearings lasted about one month during which time Judge Torres exhibited little tolerance of the seven defendants and made rulings which usually reflected the wishes of the District Attorney. Justice Edwin Torres was an intelligent literate man who was a published author of two crime novels, "Q and A" and "Carlitto's Way." He grew up in East Harlem and was very familiar with the street scene there. His parents had emigrated from Puerto Rico but he was raised in the United States. Judge Torres was an assistant prosecutor with the Office of the District in Manhattan for several years and a defense attorney before he was elevated to the bench. He had many friends in show business including Harvey Keitel who was a court stenographer in Manhattan when Judge Torres worked as an assistant District Attorney. Al Pacino had also consulted with him on a couple of his movies. First and foremost, Judge Torres usually handed out the stiffest sentences that the law allowed. When my attempts to bargain a better deal for Hylton failed, I knew that without a doubt she was going to spend at least the next twenty-five years in jail.

Before any testimony was taken we had to figure out where to seat Selma Price. The court officers concluded that because of her size, she could not fit behind the defense table in the well of the courtroom. The only place that would accommodate her overwhelming size was in the front row bench in the public seating area usually reserved for attorneys and the media. Security is paramount in any courtroom so it was necessary to surround Price with three court officers while she was in the courtroom. I hesitate to use the word "surround" when describing the position of the court officers. One was in the second row directly behind her while two others were seated on the bench along each side of her. If she were able to move at all, I could envision Price rolling over her security detail in one motion and making a clean getaway out the back door. The remaining six defendants and their lawyers, including me, were seated around the long table in the well of the court. That conflagration also included Price's attorney, the late, legendary, Joe Phillips.

Immediately, we all realized that a loose cannon was on the deck when Philips rose in defense of his client. I dislike disparaging the departed. They can't defend themselves but much of his behavior reflected badly on the other defendants and the court process itself. He would repeatedly ask inane questions and engage in nonsensical diatribes in support of his equally incomprehensible legal arguments. When he realized that the rest of us were trying to distance ourselves from him, he would attempt to win back our approval with what he considered humor. When his jokes were met with a roll of the eyes or complete silence, he would laugh at them himself while attempting to add emphasis to his comic genius by covering his mouth in a feigned attempt to hold back laughter. This would inevitably result in a violent shaking of his upper torso which lent validity to one of the basic laws of physics. For every absurd action, there is an equally absurd reaction.

Phillips lived either in the same building or next to the building where Judge Torres lived. One morning he saw Torres getting into his car to drive to court. Phillips chided Torres on the record for not offering him a ride. One time when he was an assistant prosecutor in Manhattan upon completing a trial involving the prosecution of a group of Black Panthers, he waived his duty to make a summation. He told the jury that he had done such a good job that he didn't need to make a summation. The Panthers were acquitted. I think you get the picture. If Phillips acted like that in front of her jury, it would have been the final nail in Donna Hylton's coffin. Fortunately Judge Torres solved the problem by severing Selma Price from the trial phase using a legal technicality. Price had made statements to the police against the others therefore she could not be tried in front of the same jury as her codefendants. But, so did Donna Hylton and she was not severed. Torres saw a legal way to get rid of the problems of Price and Philips for what would be a long trial. None of us complained. Price later pleaded guilty to a lesser charge and died in prison.

The skirmishes between Judge Torres and Joe Phillips were merely prologue. The drama of the testimony unfolding in the courtroom was almost secondary to the battles between myself and Judge Torres and the judge and William "Ted" Martin, the attorney for Rita Peters. When the month-long hearings concluded, it was already the beginning of December and with the holidays approaching it was decided to adjourn the trial until after the first of the year. Torres would need some time to issue an opinion as to the admissibility of the evidence and we did not want to start a trial and then interrupt it while everyone was enjoying the holidays. Before we adjourned, I asked Judge Torres if he was going to keep the case for trial or send it to another judge which is a common practice in the New York courts. He told me that he was not going to keep it which would afford me the opportunity to squeeze a short trial of long standing into my schedule before starting Hylton's trial.

On the first day back after the holidays, I started picking a jury in the case I was trying to squeeze in. As I was selecting a jury, I was summoned to Judge Torres's courtroom and asked the reason why I had ignored the starting date for Donna Hylton's trial and started another one? I politely reminded him of our conversation when we had adjourned in December. He said nothing and called the supervising judge who ordered me to stop my trial and start Hylton's case. I looked foolish and didn't protest but I did store it my long-term memory for possible use later in the trial. I then asked Judge Torres for a copy of his opinion and decision concerning the hearings. What all the attorneys got were two lines on a piece of paper denying the defense motions and permitting the District Attorney a free hand as to the introduction of evidence.

Judge Torres was never known to suffer from the stress and fatigue of overwork but this was theater of the absurd. He did this intentionally in order to escape appellate scrutiny. There would be no fact finding, no legal precedent, and no conclusions of law which might have given rise to legal error and no way to retrieve it. Just two sentences. I was dismayed that any jurist would cynically manipulate any case in such a manner, much less a murder case. I was angry for my client who would be deprived of her right to a level playing field in a trial for her life. Hylton like any other defendant, is entitled to a fair trial. At the onset of her trial for Murder in the Second Degree, one of her basic rights had already been significantly eroded.

Shortly after a jury had been picked, I filed an emergency petition with the Appellate Division to stop the proceedings until Judge Torres had issued a written opinion. The Appellate court denied my petition but at least a record had been made of Torres's attempt to shield himself from appellate scrutiny. This infuriated the judge to such an extent that he pulled me aside and informed me that he considered my reasoning in the filing of the petition fatuous. I replied that I was a fatuous little kid, but I have since lost weight. My tenuous relationship with Judge Torres was further strained when I requested a one day leave to be with my father in Syracuse who was undergoing a heart valve replacement. Torres hesitated when I asked but I told him in no uncertain terms that I was going to be with my father whether he consented or not. He said nothing further and the next morning I was at the hospital with my father. The trial continued in my absence with special instructions to the jury. There was no witness testimony concerning my client during my absence but I did ask my colleagues to be attentive if there was. Fortunately, my father survived and lived for another fourteen years.

My clashes with Judge Torres were mere child's play when compared to his clashes with Ted Martin, Rita Peter's lawyer. When we would object to one of the District Attorney's questions, Judge Torres would invariably refuse our demands for an explanation or provide a legal reason, Ted Martin would jump out of his seat and start a heated dialogue with the judge about making a proper record. These arguments grew louder and more heated as the trial wore on. Martin was not used to being in a trial with Judge Torres but the rest of us were. We would all join in Ted's argument but we made him our point man whenever an argument started. One of Torres's favorite ploys was to overrule an objection and then announce his reason later in the hope that we would forget. I always made a list of the unanswered objections and at the end of the day I would request an explanation. Torres would simply walk off the bench without uttering a sound.

Most days during trial, Martin would abruptly leave his seat and exit the courtroom without permission sometimes in the middle of testimony. When he returned he was feistier than when he had left. His clashes with Torres would become louder and had a sharper edge. I thought perhaps Ted had a bladder problem or went out for an order of sushi. But as these unannounced breaks became more frequent, I suspected there was a more sinister reason. I was particularly concerned about the change of intensity upon his return. My suspicions grew into doubt during one of our official breaks when the court reporter held his index finger against his nose and made a few snorting sounds. Evidently, he had seen something in the men's room during one of the breaks and had drawn the same conclusion. I can't say what exactly Martin was doing during the unofficial breaks but I can say that he did a hell of a job for his client throughout the trial.

The trial featured an avalanche of evidence which suffocated the defense. Courtesy of Donna Hylton, the prosecution was able to paint a vivid picture of the kidnapping plot from its inception to its tragic conclusion. They had all the names, dates, places and chronological order of events and the roles of each of the players which unfolded like a Greek tragedy. These master criminals left a trail of evidence so clear that it would have rivaled the trail left by Hansel and Gretel on their walk through the woods with the wicked witch of the west. They presented the written note used to make the recording of the ransom demand with Peter's fingerprint affixed to it. Then they presented the actual cassette in the recorder used to make the ransom demand. No one had ever bothered to remove the tape from the recorder during all the time from when it was made until the day of the arrest. It was still in the rear of the white van and never removed until the police seized it when Hylton showed up at the rental agency to reclaim her deposit. They found a notebook of instructions written by Lou the troll as well as articles of clothing belonging to the defendants also in the van. I don't know whether Hylton was going to take these items with her when she returned the van but it seemed more likely that she had resigned herself to her fate and was just trying to get rid of the van and everything in it and not think about the consequences. Vigliarolo was dead and the whole scheme to become rich and famous had blown up in her face.

The most dramatic part of the District Attorney's direct case was the testimony of the detective who had opened the steamer trunk. He described the overwhelming stench and Vigliarolo's contorted, rotting corpse in such vivid detail that it made all of us sick to our stomachs. Then he went over to the trunk, which was situated in the well of the court near to the jury, opened it gave it a soft kick.

"It still stinks," he said.

We were all in silent agreement with him. Another detective's testimony was memorable not for its content but for its laser like precision as to dates, exact times and even voucher numbers used to catalogue the evidence. He never needed to refer to his notes because everything was in the front of his brain. He was the human tape recorder and was said to have a photographic memory but to me he was more of a savant idiot who needed someone to dress him each morning. But, he was an extremely effective witness who impressed the jury with his sideshow memory. The only relief we got from the onslaught of evidence each day was from Lou the troll's lawyer the late Jim Benard whose comic imitations of his client keep us in stitches. The tall, handsome well-dressed Jim Benard and the ugly, dog-faced troll. It was a contrast you could find only in a child's book of fairy tales. The comic contrast nearly turned the trial into a tragic comedy but it helped all of us to keep our sanity.

At the close of evidence, we gave our summations. I could hardly think of what to say especially since the defense had presented no evidence. It would have been impossible to have any of the defendants try to explain away all the evidence which had flowed like Niagara from the witness stand. None of them testified upon being advised by counsel that their testimony would make it that much easier for the jury to convict them if you could imagine that. I fantasized that Lou Miranda, half human, half troll would call upon his human side and take the blame for all the misanthropy he had generated. If that were to happen, I was prepared to hire a publicist and sell tickets in front of the courthouse. I had no viable option except to attack the credibility of the prosecution's witnesses which was laughable but I did it anyway trying my best to keep a straight face when looking directly at the jury. In the midst of my summation, I decided to place all of the blame for my client's predicament on Miranda, Talag and Pace. I even blamed Selma Price for being so obese that she was physically unable to pick up the phone to notify the police. I told them that Woody Pace was a true criminal who inflicted all the pain and suffering endured by Tom Vigliarolo before it ended in that makeshift coffin. I blamed Talag for luring Donna Hylton into the plot by lying to her about advancing her career in show business. There had also been evidence of Talag's questionable character in the form of gay sadomasochistic literature discovered in her apartment when it was searched by the police.

I saved my special vitriol for Lou Miranda the architect of the misguided plot. Calling upon my Sicilian background, I described Lou the troll as a "capo di tutti capi," the boss of all bosses, my voice dripping with sarcasm as if he were a modern day Al Capone. The pathetic creature in front of them had no reaction to my words but I knew that he had understood them as did Judge Torres who grew up in East Harlem when it was mostly an Italian neighborhood and commonly used Italian slang when expressing his frustration. I concluded my summation by pointing out that Donna Hylton was the only one of the conspirators who tried to help Tom Vigliarolo despite the possibility of retaliation from Miranda and Woody Pace. Finally, I told the jury that she had fully cooperated with the police pointing out that she tried to make amends for what had happened for a disaster not of her own making. Unfortunately, I could not explain away the white van, so I conveniently ignored it. The prosecutor did not and went on to indicate that the van was a centerpiece of the plot and Hylton's role in the rental and operation of the vehicle. The District Attorney's summation lasted more than three hours and extended well past the lunch hour. I was so hungry that I was reduced to sucking on my thumb to assuage the pain in my stomach.

It was well into the next day before the jury reached its verdict. All of them were convicted of Murder in the Second Degree and Kidnapping in the First Degree. The jury had determined that each of them were acting together in the kidnapping and all of them were responsible for Vigliarolo's death even though only Miranda, Pace and Talag had actually engaged in the torture and deprivation which had led to his demise. The legal theory is designated as "acting in concert." A few weeks later each of them were sentenced to the maximum of twenty-five years to life.

My professional relationship with Judge Torres continued for many years after the Donna Hylton case. One homicide case in particular stands out in my mind as an example how we all evolve and opinions change. Several years later one of my clients who went on trial for murder was convicted of the lesser crime of manslaughter. I expected that Torres would hand down the maximum sentence of twenty-five years but he surprisingly chose a more mid-range number which I thought was imminently fair given the evidence. I also thought that his rulings reflected a more introspect analysis rather than the "shoot from the hip" attitude he exhibited in the Hylton case. But the maximum sentence given to Donna Hylton has always resonated with me as vindictiveness triumphing over reason. She should have been given a sentence closer to the minimum which was fifteen years to life for her cooperation with the police and her attempts to comfort Tom Vigliarolo as he was dying. In the criminal justice system, both factors are a legitimate consideration in determining sentence just as much as determining who pulled the trigger in a multiple defendant murder case. The same could be said of Theresa Holland. Her lawyer,

Hersh Katz, an old friend from the Legal Aid Society, argued passionately for the minimum emphasizing her foolish naïveté and lack of mental awareness in believing that her participation in the plot was a stepping stone to a modeling career. If anyone can be said to be the least guilty in this tragedy, it was Theresa Holland.

That was in 1986. For the lawyers who are still with us, there has always been some connection to the case over the decades. Unfortunately, only three out of the original seven survive. Besides Joe Phillips, Fred Seligman (who represented Marie Talag), Stanley Thomas (who represented Woody Pace and Big Jim Benard) have all passed on to their final judgment. Even the young Assistant District Attorney who assisted the lead prosecutor died of AIDS a few years later. I especially miss Jim Benard whose hilarious imitations of his client kept us entertained during the breaks. Jim was a first amendment lawyer who represented many of the owners of the porn stores which once proliferated the Times Square area. The prosecution was always obligated to turn over copies of the subject matter to the defense which formed the basis of the offense, usually in the form of films and magazines.

Jim would come up to me and say, "Well Richard, I have to go to my office to do some research into my cases."

I would reply "Do you mean you actually get paid to watch that stuff?"

In the same breath, I would offer to help him with his research. He would give me a wink and declare that it was vitally necessary for him to do all the research to be prepared as well as possible in defense of his client's constitutional rights.

William "Ted" Martin became a judge a few years later. He was on the bench for a very short time before he was indicted for tax evasion and forced to step down. There was always an undercurrent of drug involved in that indictment which was never proven. Ted was permitted to plead guilty to a misdemeanor and was suspended from the practice of law for several years during which time he did social work in the Bronx. He's still a great attorney and has a successful practice in Brooklyn. Hersh Katz and I are still plugging away at our jobs mostly in Manhattan. Justice Edwin Torres retired several years ago and as far as I know, has not authored any more books.

Several years ago, I received a phone call from an Assistant District Attorney in Brooklyn inquiring about Donna Hylton. He wanted to know if I still had any part of her file. I told him that I did not but then he started asking me questions about her trial. I asked him if he was conducting an investigation or was considering charging Hylton with a crime. He told me that he had been married to her for a very short time before she had gotten involved with the kidnapping plot and she had asked him to help her gain an early parole. I was speechless. I knew Hylton had a daughter but she never told me that she had been married much less to an ex-husband who now worked as a prosecutor.

When I told Judge Torres about the phone call, he said, "You can't make this stuff up."

My exact sentiments. During her incarceration, Hylton married one of her pen pals who later was convicted of sexually abusing her young daughter. What a train wreck of a life.

A couple of years ago I got an email from Hersh Katz about Theresa Holland. He had received information from an attorney in Rochester who was working on behalf of Holland who had been consistently denied parole after everyone else including Woody Pace has been released. The reason being that Holland has consistently refused to attend sex rehabilitation classes in prison having to do with her participation in the abuse of Tom Vigliarolo. Both Hersh and I wrote letters on her behalf emphasizing her limited intelligence and ability to be easily manipulated. I also chided the Board for releasing a degenerate like Marie Talag while refusing parole to a comparative innocent like Holland. Hersh asked Judge Torres to write a letter on Holland's behalf. After thirty years, he declined. Holland is still in jail.

I saved the fate of Lou Miranda for last. He was released by an even greater authority than the parole board. The tragedy he had orchestrated had no consequence for him. He died of heart disease about two years after his conviction and had been terminally ill when he devised his maniacal scheme. Lou the troll had gotten his revenge and had the last laugh on all of us.

IX. The Night The Music Died

The bloodiest and most violent crime scene I ever witnessed had to do with the body of a young, upper middle-class woman from the suburbs of Connecticut named Brenda Isaacs. Brenda was a young, very attractive Afro-American woman who was raised in a professional household but was tragically attracted to the bright lights and fast life of the big city. She lived in an apartment building on the west side of Manhattan in the theater district populated by theater people not far from Lincoln Center. Brenda had a proper upbringing but found herself hanging out with a group of young women who specialized in fraud and chicanery but always with a beautiful smile.

Isaacs particularly enjoyed the music scene in the New York nightclubs and was attracted to the musicians who entertained her. One warm night in the summer of 1988, Isaacs and her friends visited a now defunct nightclub called Sweetwaters which was located on Eleventh Avenue around sixty-eighth street not all that far from her apartment and close to the back entrance to the Metropolitan Opera at Lincoln Center. The club featured jazz and rhythm and blues and on that occasion, the once famous group, Harold Melvin and the Bluenotes, were booked for the entire weekend. The Bluenotes featured a blend of blues and Motown sung in perfect harmony. The group had once been very popular and had a loyal fan base among all races and ethnicities. They recorded several records which had been listed on all the popular music charts in the 1960s and 1970s but by 1988 Melvin and the Bluenotes had a very significantly reduced fan base and were on the leeward side of their careers. Still they were popular enough to draw a large audience of largely older Afro-Americans into a small nightclub.

The Bluenotes had a drummer named Carlos Railey, who was from Philadelphia as were Melvin and the other members of the group. Railey was basically a self-taught musician who had a very good reputation as a sideman for other record groups and was called upon many times to provide his skills in the studio for them. He told me that the groups could always depend on him to show up because he never used drugs. Railey had been a member of the Bluenotes on and off for a number of years but could barely make enough money to feed himself much less the four or five children had fathered out of wedlock. He told me that he, Melvin and the rest of the Bluenotes once piled into their van with their instruments and drove all the way from Philly to Detroit lured on by Melvin's promise of a big pay day. At the end of their weekend gig, each of them received a whopping fifty dollars for their trouble. Railey had been injured in a fire when he was a child and had been terribly scarred on both his legs from the knees to the ankles. He also had lost the use of two of his fingers on his left hand. This added to the mystique a well-regarded drummer being able to perform at a high level having use of only eight of his ten fingers. Both these factors would become very significant in the death of Brenda Isaacs. Railey's disability put me in mind of the great Gypsy jazz guitarist Django Reinhardt who had lost the use of two of his fingers in a similar way. Reinhardt became a legend and Railey had become quite proficient given a similar disability.

Isaacs and her friends sat up front near the stage on this fateful night so they could flirt with the musicians. She caught the eye of the group's drummer and she and Railey struck up a conversation between sets which continued throughout the night until closing. It was about two in the morning and Railey was tired and knew that he would not make it back to Philadelphia in the van for several hours because Harold Melvin had to make his usual drug stops in New Jersey. He convinced Isaacs to let him stay in her apartment on the west side so he could get a good night's sleep instead of waiting for Melvin to make his drug connections. Unfortunately, her casual acquiescence to a one night's stay meant a one-night stand to Carlos Railey and this is where the plot thickened.

Railey went back to the apartment and, according to him, they talked and had something to eat. No confidences violated here because he told the police pretty much the same thing and it was recorded and later admitted into evidence. Railey knew that somehow Brenda Isaacs was involved with the drug trade because the group of young women she hung out with had that reputation. He was told by Melvin that the group sold stolen furs on the street sometimes right in front of Sweetwaters. He had never met Isaacs before but he did know some of the other women and was not surprised by what happened in the apartment shortly after they had arrived. Isaacs received a phone call and Railey was told to leave the room. He decided to go into the bathroom but he did overhear what police undercover officers call "a drug related conversation" before he entered. While in the bathroom he heard the down stairs front doorbell ring in her apartment. New York City apartments are equipped with an intercom system which permits the tenants to speak to the person attempting to gain entrance to the building and buzzer system which rings them in. He heard Isaacs go over to the intercom to ring in her visitor. This occurred just a few minutes after the telephone conversation. At this point, he decided to take a shower but he did hear the muffled sounds of Isaacs speaking with a man in the apartment while he was taking his shower.

Railey continued with his shower for about fifteen minutes and when he turned it off, he heard Isaac's television playing very loudly but no longer heard the muffled voices. He passed a few more minutes in the bathroom drying himself before venturing back into the bedroom where he had last seen Brenda Isaacs. When he turned the corner into the bedroom, Railey said that he saw a vision of hell. Brenda Isaacs was laying on her bed with entire left side ripped open from her face to her left breast but was still breathing and aspirating blood. I saw the crime scene video and it seemed that poor Brenda had been filleted like a large fish with its entrails hanging out. The left side of her face was cut opened to the bone and her left eyeball dangled precariously on her left cheekbone attached only by a tendon to what was left of her eye socket. Her face had been excavated to such an extent that her jawbone with rear molars, partially severed tongue, broken eye socket and cheekbone, sinus cavity and parts of her inner ear along with the dangling eyeball were plainly visible to the naked eye. Her left breast and chest wall were also slashed open and there was a man's leather belt tied in the form of a garrote around her neck which had also been cut open but not as extensively as the face. This had been a murder fueled by intense passion and was very personal in nature. The assailant most likely had an intimate relationship with the victim.

Railey told me and the police that he was wearing a white t-shirt and underwear when he discovered Brenda's almost lifeless body. He had wanted to retrieve his trousers which were on her bed but he discovered that they were folded up under her body and soaked in blood. Isaacs had lost so much blood that it saturated through to the mattress and covered nearly her entire upper torso. The white t-shirt was found to have blood on it and Railey said that Isaac's was gurgling blood which was sprayed onto it when he bent over to get close enough to her face to see if she was still breathing. He said that whatever happened to her had taken place while he was in the bathroom and that he had heard nothing besides the ringing apartment bell and the muffled sound of a male voice just as he was about to take his shower. DNA testing was still in its infancy and a relatively unused procedure in 1988, so only blood typing was performed and the testimony of blood stain experts would be tantamount.

Railey said that he panicked when he realized that Brenda Isaacs was probably dead and he rushed out of her apartment wearing her bathrobe and his blood-stained shoes, hailed a cab and could only think of going back to Sweetwaters for help. It was about 9:00 AM when he arrived at the club and since this was a night club, it was not unexpectedly closed. He looked through the glass door and saw his drum set which was still on the stage and then knocked several times until one of the club's custodians came to the door. The custodian was reluctant to open the door to unknown man dressed somewhat like a woman with blood on his shoes asking to use the phone. Railey pointed to his drum set on the stage and the custodian finally opened the door. He phoned the police who told him to wait for them on the sidewalk in front of the club. Several minutes later, the police picked him up, bathrobe and all, and they journeyed the twenty blocks south to view the horrific scene in Brenda Isaacs's apartment.

He told the police essentially the same story as I have described but they arrested Railey and charged him with murder. The police gave some credence to his story but were obliged to arrest him especially after they saw his blood-soaked trousers and the bone-dry bathtub less than an hour after Railey said he had taken his shower. The police processed him through central booking and he was brought to arraignment court where I had been working on that same day. When I first met Railey he had been in custody for about thirty-six hours mostly being debriefed by the detectives. During that period, he had prevailed upon one of the other Bluenotes to bring some his clothes so that he would not appear in court wearing Isaac's bathrobe. But, the word was out in Philly and by that time the police had shown Harold Melvin pictures of Brenda Isaacs's mutilated torso, Railey would receive no further help from Melvin or any of the other Bluenotes.

It was a Monday when Railey was brought to arraignment court and the murder had occurred sometime in the early morning hours of Saturday. He told me essentially the same story and really didn't look too bad considering what he had just been through. When I was finished with my initial interview, I approached the Assistant District Attorney who was working the arraignment part and inquired if the police had done any preliminary investigation into Railey's claims of another man in the apartment during the time he had been in the bathroom. Ordinarily, I would ask the assistant if they were going to request bail and how much. In this case it was a homicide which invariably results in a remand status with no possibility of posting bail . I never bothered to broach the subject with the assistant but to my utter shock and surprise, he told me that his office was going to consent to Railey's release pending formal indictment. This was never done in a murder case and I thought that the stars were in perfect alignment but it probably had to do more with the plausible story he had told and the police were still investigating his allegations. As it turned out that assumption was correct.

Railey was brought out of the holding pen area to a bench inside the well of the courtroom which afforded him an opportunity to look out over the public area where any interested citizen can sit. He was seated and handcuffed behind his back awaiting his formal appearance before the judge when suddenly he attracted my attention by gesturing with his head indicating that he wanted to talk to me. His eyes grew wide and he looked frightened. He told me that a couple of sinister looking black men sitting about five or six rows back from the front were friends of the deceased and that he was convinced that his life would be in danger if they were still in the area upon his release. Railey's case was about to be called when I approached the judge and asked to speak with him at the bench where we could not be heard by the audience. I positioned myself in front of the judge so that he could look directly over my right shoulder to see where the two men were sitting. I explained the situation to him using my concealed index finger to point out the two potential malevolents in the audience behind me. The judge took one look and agreed to call a luncheon recess and clear the courtroom before Railey was released. The audience was told that the courtroom would be locked until 2:15 PM when the afternoon session would begin. We waited a few minutes and court officers were sent into the public corridor to determine whether the two men had left the area. The all clear was signaled and Railey was arraigned and released to an empty courtroom and a staff that had worked an extra ten minutes beyond their lunch break.

Railey and I walked together through the first-floor corridor of the courthouse toward the main exit but the closer we got to the door, the closer Railey got to my left shoulder. When we got to the stairs leading to the sidewalk I discovered that he had lagged behind by about two feet and he had positioned himself almost directly behind me. I asked him to get next to me because I was trying to have a conversation with him and that I wasn't an owl with the ability to turn my head 180 degrees. He responded by getting closer to my shoulder and lowering his whole body so that my body formed an almost perfect barrier to his. It didn't take a genius to figure out that Railey intended me to take the first bullet when the shooting started. I stepped away from him as I was becoming a little apprehensive myself. I asked him where he was going to stay. He said that he had no place to stay except with his mother in Philadelphia but that he had no money to get there. Remembering the faces of the two thugs in the courtroom that we had temporarily outwitted, I reached for my wallet pulled out a couple of twenties, handed them to him and told him to get to Penn Station as fast as the nearest cab could take him and not to return to New York until he heard from me. As he was getting into the cab, I told him that he made almost as much money from me as he did for the whole weekend gig in Detroit.

I went back to my office with a sandwich that I had purchased with money borrowed from a colleague because I had given all my cash to Railey. I rationalized my impoverished state that had reduced me to begging because I thought that my life was worth a little more than forty dollars. I contacted my investigator Leroy Witherspoon and excitedly told him of my great adventure leaving arraignment court. Spoon, who had been a cop for almost thirty years, laughed and called me a rookie and not to repeat the story to any of his ex-cop investigator friends because they would laugh at me too. I had called Spoon to engage his services for Carlos Railey's case. Leroy Wither-spoon had retired from the New York City Police Department as a very highly regarded detective first grade. He was one of the handful of detectives chosen from around the country to help solve the Atlanta child murders which had plagued that city in the late 1970s. Spoon was on the case before Railey had been formally charged. It was very prophetic that Spoon had added to his impressive resume by being chosen to investigate the Atlanta murders. Our greatest adventure together with the Carlos Railey case had to do with the city of Atlanta.

Railey was indicted for Murder in the Second Degree about a month after his initial court appearance. By that time the Connecticut newspapers had gotten wind of the savage murder of one of their residents and an entourage of reporters from that state's newspapers were waiting for us when I escorted Railey to the courtroom. I managed to help Railey navigate the bevy of reporters and flash cameras until we reached the outer door of the courtroom when we encountered a particularly obnoxious cameraman who tried to shove his camera right in Railey's face. He was short, potbellied and it looked like he hadn't changed his clothes in a week. What stood out when you saw him was his greasy thinning hair and his flat feet, which were regaled in the most garish hi-top basketball sneakers you ever laid your eyes on. The color accentuated the fact that the standing position of his feet ran east-west instead of north-south. This time I had told Railey to walk behind me and hide his face. This did not deter the cameraman with the Valvoline hair. He tried to push me out of the way to get a clearer view of Railey. I responded by licking my index finger and rubbing it on his lens. He called me an asshole and added that he was only doing his job. I told him that his whole body needed to be dipped in disinfectant then Railey and I pushed our way passed him into the courtroom. With cameras not allowed in the courtrooms in those days, it would be the last chance the media would have to take a picture of Railey as a free man.

The District Attorney requested and received a significant increase in bail conditions to one hundred thousand dollars. The bail was set by the late Justice Alvin Williams who was a fair and considerate man. He could have remanded Railey with no possibility of bail but he took into consideration Railey's voluntary return to court after being released on a capital charge and the fact that he had no criminal record whatsoever. Railey was put in jail and the cameramen outside the courtroom were bitterly disappointed when I emerged and announced that if they wanted a picture of Carlos Railey they would have to contact the Department of Corrections. The family attempted to raise the money necessary to get him out of jail all through his incarceration but their efforts fell short. It was time for Leroy Witherspoon and me to work our magic in defense of Carlos Railey. Little did we know how difficult that would be?

We were interested in learning more about Brenda Isaacs's life. The police had already canvassed her apartment building but Spoon went back to knock on a few doors on the same floor. Evidently, she had led a quiet life there and we gathered no useful information using that strategy. Then we tried to locate some of the group of young women named by Railey who were allegedly involved with drugs and stolen furs. We had only first names or nicknames but Spoon managed to locate two of them. One managed a kiosk at JFK Airport selling travel insurance and the other ran a store which specialized in expensive fur coats in, of all places, Atlanta, Georgia. Railey had told us that he had a brief weekend interlude with her several months earlier when the Bluenotes were playing in that city. Spoon and I thought this was a curiously familiar scenario but we put this information on the back burner until we had gone to Connecticut to interview Brenda Isaacs's family.

We thought that we would never get passed the front door of Brenda Isaacs's parents' home but, as usual, Spoon thought of a gimmick which might get us in. Spoon had worked with a detective who had retired to the same town in Connecticut so he contacted him and as luck would have it, he was a friend of the Isaacs. Spoon arranged with the former detective to have us meet with Brenda Isaacs's mother with the detective present. Surprisingly enough, Brenda's mother was very cordial and was willing to answer most of our questions. We learned the last names of some of her daughter's friends but no addresses. She did say that her daughter had stars in her eyes about becoming a model and that she ran around with a fast crowd but her daughter was not forthcoming about her life in New York City. We had cast some doubt in her mind about Railey's guilt by telling her that her daughter may have been the innocent victim of one of her friend's bad drug deals. She seemed skeptical, but Spoon and I thought we had come upon a theory which seemed as plausible as Railey's story to the police and that was the reason she was so cooperative. As the case unfolded, she became increasingly uncooperative and told us that she thought Railey's story was a fairy tale.

Our next stop was the travel insurance kiosk at JFK Airport. Spoon had suspected that the word was out that we were looking for Brenda's friends. His doubts were confirmed when we could no longer dig up any more information as to her friends including the manager of the insurance kiosk who had recently quit her job leaving no forwarding information. We thought that Railey's belief that Isaacs was involved with a criminal enterprise was accurate. Our leads suddenly dried up as the witnesses disappeared as soon as we discovered their addresses. I thought of the two thugs who were waiting for Railey to exit the courtroom and when I reminded Spoon of the incident, he was convinced we would never find Isaacs's friends and if we did, they would stonewall us. I agreed but we did know the name and general location of Railey's one-night stand in Atlanta. But there was one more stop we had to make before venturing to Atlanta.

Railey had told us the address of Harold Melvin and his family in the Mount Airy section of Philadelphia. Melvin would have nothing to do with Railey after the police had shown him the horrific photos of Brenda Isaacs's body. We wanted to speak particularly with Melvin's wife and daughter who had socialized with Railey for many years, but we had to do it when Melvin was out of the house. One of Railey's friends had visited him in jail and told him that the Bluenotes were going to Kansas City for a two-week engagement. We chose this time to go to Philadelphia to make an unannounced visit to the home of Harold Melvin. Fortunately, Mrs. Melvin was home when we knocked on the door and her daughter arrived a short time later. The Melvins could not have been more cordial to us but Mrs. Melvin told us on no uncertain terms that we would not have made it passed the front door if her husband had been around. We were interested in learning more about our client and whether Harold had said anything to the police about Railey when shown the photos.

Mrs. Melvin was effusive in her praise of Railey but her husband had not discussed his meeting with the police with her. He did tell about viewing the pictures but he did not wish to speak any further of them. Mrs. Melvin could not believe Railey would commit such a horrendous crime. We asked about her husband's life on the road. She responded that her husband rarely discussed his life outside of the home. She knew that her husband had abused drugs in the past they had gone through an intervention and she believed that her husband no longer used drugs. "Spouses and parents are always the last to know," I thought silently. She added that she never saw Railey use drugs nor had she heard any gossip to that effect. The Melvin's daughter also thought highly of Railey and could add nothing about his personal life. We left after about two hours with the promise that our meeting would remain a secret among the four of us.

The time had come to plan our trip to Atlanta. Spoon and I thought that it would yield the most information. The problem was that we had only the name and a picture of the young woman who ran the fur store and had the weekend tryst with Railey. He could not remember the address or even the street but he did remember that she lived in a large apartment building with a doorman. It was difficult for Spoon to find the time to go to Atlanta but we managed to squeeze in our trip on a summer weekend in August. When we got to Atlanta, we immediately went to the main police station where Spoon flashed his detective badge and requested information concerning the fur store and its proprietress. He told the Atlanta police that he was one of the detectives who had helped in the child murder case a decade before and they responded by opening their files. We discovered that the fur store had been burglarized under suspicious circumstances about a year prior and the insurance company had attempted to locate the young proprietress after they had paid the claim but without success. The insurance money had been sent to the store address and shortly thereafter it was closed and the proprietress could not be located. Spoon thanked his colleagues in Atlanta and we decided to drive our compact rental around until we could locate a large apartment building that matched Railey's description.

While exploring the city we determined that there were only three apartment buildings in the downtown area which would qualify as being considered large. We drove to the nearest building and as luck would have it, we struck gold. When we got to the front door Spoon noticed that the doorman in the lobby was a brother. He told me to stay in the car explaining that the doorman would get nervous if he saw a white dude standing next to him when he was asking questions. Before he got out of the car, Spoon asked me to give him a few "saw bucks" or more specifically, two ten-dollar bills, and with a grin on his face he made his way to the front desk where his "bro," the doorman, was located.

I parked the car out of sight and waited for Spoon to work his magic. He returned about fifteen minutes later and told me that he had shown the picture of our person of interest to the doorman. He then told me, with a look of exasperation, that he had "lost" the two ten-dollar bills. I asked him how in the hell did that happen? He responded that he laid one bill on the desk in front of the doorman and it had somehow fallen behind the desk and neither of them could find it. Spoon then gave him the other ten-dollar bill indicating that he could keep that one if he found the other.

My look of skepticism made him laugh and then he said, "Oh by the way, she lives in apartment 5-C but didn't pick up when we rang her phone."

We had discovered her location in about a half hour what the insurance investigators were trying to determine for at least a whole year.

It was the mid-afternoon on Saturday when this occurred and we returned to the apartment building three more times that day. The last time was about eight in the evening but there was no response to our calls. Since it was Saturday night, we figured that she would not return, if at all, until well past our bedtimes. In between our unsuccessful visits, we visited the now shuttered fur salon. The windows had been papered over from the inside but there were gaps big enough to see through to the entire area long since devoid of expensive furs. There was a large section of the wall adjoining the empty store area next door which looked like it had been plastered over but left unpainted. The obvious alternate entrance for those not possessing a key to the front door. We went around to the back and discovered that the emergency exit door had a panic bar which would probably have set off an alarm when opened. In those days, surveillance cameras were not as popular as they are now, so we surmised that it could have very easily been an inside job with the thieves simply entering the front door most likely with a key, knocking through the wall as a subterfuge and then exiting the back after disengaging the alarm. I do declare that it would be very easy to throw those lovely fur coats into a rented van and drive nonstop from the land of southern comfort to the crush of New York City.

We went back to our motel around 9 PM after our last visit to the apartment building. Spoon had a cousin in the area who suggested the names of a few bars that were popular with the Afro-American community where we could combine business with pleasure. Spoon nixed the idea telling me that for once in my life I was the wrong color and if we were seen together, the denizens of the bar would think that we were cops and clam up. It might even get a little tense since we would probably be the only mixed couple in an all-black environment. We spent the evening watching the Atlanta Braves on television, said our prayers and went to bed early. We intended to get up early and stake out the apartment building until our quarry had returned. It was Sunday and we had plane reservations early that evening for our return to the Big Apple. We did not want to return empty handed so we were prepared to wait all day.

We arose very early the next morning and went across the street to a well-known fast food restaurant for an unhealthy breakfast. Spoon, who basically lived on black coffee, cigarettes and peanuts, ate the left-over pizza from the night before then ordered more black coffee when we got to the restaurant. We were well fortified expecting what could have been a very long wait. Our rental was the smallest, cheapest car that was available. It was called a Sunbird with max speed of about seventy-five miles per hour with a tail wind. With two grown men in tow, I was sure that the little Sunbird would have much trouble getting up to speed. I was driving which probably saved our lives. Before I could switch off the ignition, the Iron Gate to the parking garage opened and a black Chevy Beretta emerged with a young black woman at the wheel. She looked both ways before entering the roadway in front of the building which afforded us the opportunity to get a good look at the very attractive driver. We were only about twenty-five feet away when we both screamed, "That's her!"

We took off after the Beretta onto the main expressway. We followed the car as best we could. The Beretta would engage its turn signal as if to indicate that it was exiting the highway but would suddenly swerve back onto the roadway. The Beretta made this maneuver on at least three separate occasions which was one of the methods used by a drug courier trying to avoid detection. I could not imagine that our little Sunbird would be suspected of surveillance capabilities when compared to a mighty Beretta but this was a standard operating procedure when carrying contraband.

Each time the Beretta made this maneuver, the little engine that could lost power and started to overheat. Spoon was screaming that I should let him drive and I responded as to how we were supposed to accomplish this feat at seventy-five miles per hour. Soon one black Beretta became several black Berettas and we lost her in the traffic. Spoon was so excited that he started to sweat. I was surprised that he got so involved with the chase given his three decades of experience as a cop. He then told me that he should have been driving to which I responded that we would have not survived if he was behind the wheel. Besides our little Sunbird was gasping for air and we had to pull off the expressway because of the overheating problem or else the engine would have blown and left us at the mercy of the speeding traffic. He grudgingly accepted what had happened and suggested that we go back to the apartment building after a few hours to see if the black Beretta had returned to its parking spot in the garage.

We had lunch with Spoon's cousin and returned to the apartment building around 2:30 PM. This time we both walked into the lobby and the doorman greeted us like we were royalty. By this time a few more ten-dollar bills had mysteriously made their way onto the floor behind the desk and just as mysteriously been found by the doorman who we complimented for his uncanny ability to find lost treasure. I figured that the doorman was about sixty dollars richer than he would have been if we had not decided to go to Atlanta. He told us that our subject had returned to her apartment about an hour earlier. The doorman called her apartment, explained that she had visitors and handed the phone to Spoon who told her that he had come all the way from New York City and was "investigating" the death of Brenda Isaacs with his "assistant." Not once did he mention the fact that we were part of the defense team that was defending the man who was accused of gutting her friend like a fish or that I was his lawyer. She said that she knew Brenda and wanted to help.

We went upstairs and rang the apartment bell. Before she opened the door, Spoon reached into his suit jacket pocket and switched on his micro recorder. We asked about her friendship with Brenda Isaacs. She responded that she knew Brenda from New York City where she had been born and raised. We asked if she knew if Brenda was involved with drugs. She innocently said that she did not think so but could not say for sure. We never mentioned the correlation between her driving habits and our question. Then we asked her about the fur store. She said that it was necessary to close it because her silent partners refused to back her after the "burglary." Rumor had it that one of the silent partners was a hall of fame professional basketball player but she never mentioned names. Finally, we got to the real reason we were there: Carlos Railey.

When we mentioned his name, our girl rolled her eyes and gave us a look of disgust. Then she gratuitously called him "a total jerk" before we could ask another question. She went on to say that she had met Railey on more than one occasion when he was playing with the Bluenotes both in New York and Atlanta. The last time she saw him he asked to stay at her apartment for the weekend because he did not like the accommodations that had been arranged for the group by Harold Melvin. He was supposed to leave when the engagement ended but had unilaterally extended his stay because he thought that they had become "a couple." She assured him that she was just having some fun and that they were definitely not a couple. He rejected this notion and became violent when she threw his clothes into the lobby attempting to get rid of him. Railey responded by slamming her head into a wall and it took the intervention of some of her "friends" to convince Railey that it would be in his best interests to leave immediately. Sounded vaguely familiar to what might have happened to Brenda Isaacs. We concluded our interview after about an hour. It was useless to continue asking her questions she would either not answer or suffer a lapse of memory. But she had no memory lapses when it came to her weekend fling with our client. She had rendered herself useless as a witness and changed the course of our focus in the case.

When we got back to New York, I told Spoon to destroy our clandestine recording lest it somehow fell into the wrong hands. Even though the recorder was in Spoon's jacket pocket, the sound was extraordinarily clear and every word faithfully reproduced. You could almost hear the sound of her head hitting the wall as she was recounting her weekend experience with Railey. I decided that I would have to make a frontal assault on the forensic evidence in the case which was extensive. Spoon had located a couple of other friends of Brenda Isaacs but they were not about to tell us about their criminal enterprise and, of course, no one ever saw stolen fur coats being sold on the streets of Manhattan. I engaged the services of a renowned forensic expert Dr. Peter DeForest to examine Railey's white t-shirt, shoes and trousers. As a defense attorney, you always run the risk of doing too much in the defense of your client. Since the police and the District Attorney have all the evidence, you must request either an order of the court allowing your expert access or ask the District Attorney to allow it without a court order. In either case, you are tipping your hand as to the nature of your defense. It is like the fundamental rule of cross examination. If you don't know the answer beforehand, don't ask the question.

I was particularly interested in having Dr. DeForest examine Railey's t-shirt and trousers. Railey had told the police and me that he had gotten close enough to Brenda Isaacs that she had aspirated blood on his shirt as she was dying. If what Railey had told us was true, the blood spatter on his shirt should have been shone as a fine mist easily recognizable by Dr. DeForest. What he found was high intensity impact spatter which could only be formed if the shirt had come into contact with blood that had been ejected from the body upon impact by some type of trauma. A knife cutting into an artery would create this type of blood stain spatter. Next, he examined the blood-soaked trousers which were found under the body of Brenda Isaacs. Railey said that when he returned to the bedroom from the bathroom he saw that the trousers were lying in a flat position under her body and that he made no attempt to remove them. Dr. DeForest theorized that if what Railey had said was accurate, the trousers would have been soaked through front to back and some blood saturation should have been discovered on both surfaces. The only blood he found was on the front of each pant leg and was of the opinion that the reason no blood appeared on the back part of the pant legs was that there must have been an object in the hollow of each pant leg which had prevented the blood on the front from soaking through to the back.

The stunning conclusion was that there was a high degree of probability Railey was wearing his white t-shirt when the high impact blood struck its surface and it was with an equally high degree of probability that the objects in the hollow of the trousers were the legs of Carlos Railey. Dr. DeForest then told me that if he were to testify, his scientific conclusions would turn him into a witness for the prosecution and that it would be best if he issued no report of his findings. Dr. DeForest's conclusions were a dagger in the heart of the defense. My attempt to corroborate Railey's statements with forensic analysis had fallen flat on its face and resulted in the District Attorney engaging the services of Dr. Henry Lee who, four years later, would be the forensic blood stain expert in the O.J. Simpson case.

I knew that I was taking a chance but with no other defense on the horizon I had to do it in the hope that it would give some scientific credibility to Railey's version of events. I doubt that the District Attorney would have countered with a forensic scientist with the reputation of Henry Lee if I had chosen not to challenge the blood evidence. If the blood evidence had backed up Railey's story, I would have been a tactical genius. I should have sat on my hands and let the District Attorney prove their case. You pays your money and you takes your chances. Nothing Railey had told me had any basis in forensic science. I was told that the witness in Atlanta was one of his girlfriends and knew about Brenda Isaacs's drug related activities. She hated his guts and would have gladly testified as to his violent nature and would have never volunteered information about Isaacs's illegal activities which would have implicated herself not to mention the fur coat caper.

The case dragged on for about eighteen months which is not unusual for a homicide case. On one occasion, I went back to the holding pens to talk to Railey before he made his scheduled court appearance. I found him in tears and asked why. He said that he was feeling bad about what had happened to Brenda Isaacs and felt some guilt about possibly having something to do with her death. Up until this point, he had shown very little in the way of emotion. I asked him straight away if he wanted to plead guilty to the murder. He recovered quickly and said that he had nothing to do with the murder but felt bad about being there when it had happened. I said that he was lucky to be alive because murderers never leave witnesses. His tears dried up and he continued professing his innocence.

The trial started before the late Hon. Robert Haft. Judge Haft was a decent man and a fair judge. It took about three days to pick a jury. I wasn't exactly overconfident but I did think of a trial strategy which I thought might raise some reasonable doubt in the minds of at least one juror if not a few more. You'll remember that Railey had lost the use of two of his fingers in a fire when he was a child. According to the autopsy report, Brenda Isaacs's cause of death was puncture wound by stabbing and asphyxiation. A garroted belt had been found around her neck and there were ligature marks on her neck. There was petechial hemorrhaging which are tiny red spots in the eye that are formed by burst capillaries caused by suffocation. If the coroner's report was accurate, it would mean that Brenda was simultaneously strangled and stabbed.

Given Railey's infirmity, it was more likely that two individuals were involved the murder since Railey would not have the strength in one of his hands to choke and stab her at the same time. That was the defense's theory and the medical examiner agreed that this scenario was possible but added that one individual could have accomplished the same feat. Probably a long shot but worth a try since other avenues had been blocked.

I was surprised when the Assistant District Attorney assigned to the case decided not to use most of Railey's statement to the police. Some of it was admitted but the rest was either suppressed in evidence or simply discarded by the prosecution. No mean feat given the law on voluntariness. Some of his statement was legally in violation of Railey's right against self-incrimination. Other parts of it had been redacted because Railey had mentioned certain names which really had nothing to do with the case and were considered self-serving. That is the panacea of all prosecutors who wish only those parts of the statement which are most helpful to them to be admitted into evidence. To make a long story short, I had to decide as to whether I should have Railey testify in order for his entire statement to be admitted into evidence or go with what the District Attorney wanted admitted. It is never a good idea to have your client testify in his own behalf in a murder case but the judge's rulings had boxed us in and testifying had become a distinct possibility.

The trial began with the usual assortment of police witnesses who pretty much recounted the story as I have described without the names of Brenda Isaacs's friends, her reputation for being a drug courier along with her friends or the story of the great Atlanta fur shop heist. There would be no testimony regarding Railey's useless fingers since the police were not experts in that area. I had consulted with a New York doctor about Railey's fingers but he could not come to any medical conclusion as the strength of his hands given the infirmity. Railey would have to describe it himself. The police could not say whether two individuals were involved in the murder and there was no DNA testing at that time. It had not yet become the fashion in homicide investigations. The horrific photos of the crime scene were shown but only enough for the jury to get the picture of what went on in that apartment. Fortunately for the family of Brenda Isaacs, only one photo of her mutilated face and upper torso taken at a distance was shown to the jury.

What had come before was merely prelude to the appearance of Dr. Henry Lee the prosecution's star witness. Dr. DeForest had prepared me with relevant scientific questions to ask on cross examination but Dr. Lee's performance was a hard act to follow. Lee pulled out his heavy-duty sheets of pure white paper, and his eye dropper full of bright red ink. He demonstrated the effect of high velocity blood striking the surface of the heavy duty white paper by flicking the eye dropper full of red ink with his wrist simulating the speed of high velocity blood spatter. The pattern leaves a streak on the paper before coming to rest in the form of a heavier, more rounded blotch. He likened this type of pattern to a comet with a visible tail. Then, in anticipation of my cross examination, he demonstrated the difference between high velocity spatter and the pattern produced by dripping blood on the white surface. Lee reloaded his trusty eye dropper, held it over the white paper and squeezed out a drop which left a pattern which was more rounded and spread out with no comet like tail. He indicated that the blood stain spatter on Railey's t-shirt was of the high velocity nature which could only be made by the blood exiting the body at high speed. The implication being that this pattern could not have possibly been formed by aspirated or dripping blood. For some inexplicable reason, Lee was never questioned about the blood stain pattern on Railey's trousers. I never mentioned it during cross examination.

My cross examination of Dr. Lee consisted primarily of asking him if he had any tools at his disposal whereby he could demonstrate the pattern formed by aspirated blood. He explained that it would be difficult to recreate since aspirated blood contained other bodily fluids such as saliva. But he was certain of his analysis of the blood pattern on Railey's shirt. I asked him to repeat much of his direct examination in an effort to develop inconsistencies in his original testimony. This is a tactic which is used when the defense is attempting to discredit the witness's testimony commonly described as a fishing expedition. It is a tactic loathed by judges but which sometimes works. Henry Lee was steadfast in his testimony. His inscrutable eastern mind would not be changed by such a cheap trick. I imagine that he had been subjected to this tactic many times over the years because he showed an almost imperceptible smirk during most of my questioning. Taking my cue from the imperceptible smirk, I ended by cross examination by likening the red ink spots on the white background to a Caucasian with the measles. The juxtaposition of racial features was not lost on Dr. Lee. He smiled broadly and agreed.

The prosecution rested its case and it was now time to make the decision as whether Railey would take the stand and tell his story. I explained to him the potential hazard of a defendant charged with murder testifying on his own behalf. He agreed that he would have to tell the jury his version of events if he had any chance at all. I prepped him as best I could especially when he was cross examined by the prosecutor. I crossed my fingers but had that usual sinking feeling in my gut when a defendant takes the stand. I perceived Railey as presenting a relatively clean image to the jury. He had no criminal record and there was no evidence of any propensity for violence. The prosecutor had no knowledge of the Beretta driver in Atlanta. I thought that we were as properly prepared as possible. Then Railey began his testimony and all of my nightmares became reality.

I did not anticipate Railey's conscience getting in the way of all our carefully laid plans. As he began telling his story, you could see the tears welling up in his eyes. While he was saying the right things, his demeanor told a story of guilt and remorse. The beginning of his testimony went according to plan but within a short period of time the frustration caused by a lifetime of unfulfilled dreams rose to the surface. He criticized the manner in which he had been treated by Harold Melvin and the music industry in general. The implication being that his talent was not really appreciated by the rest of the world and it had become obvious to the jury and everyone else in the courtroom that Railey was filled with suppressed rage. It was a rage that could have easily exploded into violence which is exactly what should not be displayed to a group of twelve people who could send you to jail for the rest of your life.

Then he spoke of Brenda Isaacs. As he spoke of the horrific scene in the bedroom of her apartment, he began to whimper and shed tears while expressing profound sorrow as to the way in which she had died. The tears were sincere enough but it seemed obvious to everyone that they were an expression of guilt and remorse from a person trying to come to terms with what he had done. Just before Railey finished his testimony his new girlfriend whom he had met and lived with for the period of time he had been released, got up out of her seat near the front of the courtroom and walked down the aisle towards the door. She never looked back but you could tell by her body language and the noise she made as she pounded her high heels into the tile floor that she was disgusted by Railey's testimony. I never saw her again and I doubt Railey ever did either. The prosecutor cross examined him but it really wasn't necessary. Railey had convicted himself.

The jury started their deliberations in the late morning and reached a verdict by late afternoon. Railey was convicted of Murder in the Second degree and received the maximum sentence of twenty-five years to life. Spoon and I speculated that when Railey and Isaacs went to her apartment, the invitation for a night's stay meant more to him than it did to her. What ever happened in that apartment had obviously led to some type of catastrophic disagreement? Perhaps he wanted sex. Maybe she led him on but was just playing with his emotions. He became more demanding and things had gotten to the stage where he had taken off his pants and she was in a nightgown. Perhaps he had just tried to overwhelm her. We both agreed that Isaacs was put off by the burn scars on Railey's legs and may have made a derogatory statement which caused him to lose control. The slaughter of Brenda Isaacs had been the culmination of the anger and rage he had been pent-up for most of his life. The potential for extreme violence was present long before they met. Somehow Brenda Isaacs managed to push the wrong button. Railey was paroled in 2015 after serving twenty-seven years. He'll be on parole for the rest of his life.

Leroy Witherspoon died in 1999 before his time the victim of emphysema caused by a lifetime addiction to cigarettes. We had worked together on many cases over the years but none like the Carlos Railey case. At the end, Spoon could hardly walk because of his breathing difficulties. The last time I saw him was about a year before his death. He was sitting on a bench next to the parking lot across from the main Criminal Courts building in Manhattan. He told me that he was trying to reach his car but was having a bad day and was only able to walk a short distance before he had to rest. I offered to drive his car to his home in Queens but he declined saying that he had some work to do before heading home. Spoon had been buried for a couple of weeks before word reached me that he had passed. That is the way it is in New York City where hundreds of good people pass on every day without fanfare. That was the way it was with Spoon. I learned a lot from him.

X. The Vietnamese Kinnaree
Illusion And Disillusion

A Kinnaree is a figure of Southeast Asian mythology having its roots in Buddhism. The Kinnaree has the face, arms and torso of a woman while the lower torso resembles that of a bird. It has wings which allows it to easily navigate between the real and mystical worlds and is considered a symbol of great beauty and allurement. A marvelous book featuring Kinnarees and the after-effects of the Vietnam War upon returning American soldiers was written by the late Susan Bromberg Schaffer entitled *Buffalo Afternoon*. In her novel, Schaffer describes a Native American soldier unable to cope with the psychological trauma of combat in Vietnam. The soldier was in a psychiatric hospital and on the final day of his life viewed a Kinnaree hovering outside of his window beckoning him. The window was on one of the top floors of the hospital but the soldier was so enamored with the winged apparition that he followed it out of the window ending his interminable suffering.

A brief history of the Kinnaree serves as a convenient vehicle to introduce the case of The People v. Gilbert Nash. Nash had been a combat soldier during the height of the Vietnam War suffering from the effects of post-traumatic stress disorder (PTSD) for nearly twenty years when he was indicted for the murder of his older brother. He returned home with one of the worst cases of PTSD you could imagine. Nash's emotional difficulties could be traced to his childhood where he was raised in a fatherless home with other siblings and half-siblings. There was little affection and much psychological abuse. He wrote intelligently about his childhood and his experiences as a combat soldier in Vietnam. The psychological trauma he suffered as a child was merely prologue to the trauma he had endured in Vietnam.

Nash had suffered a great deal of psychological abuse at the hands of his mother when he was a child. Their relationship was tenuous at best and Nash felt as if he was the child singled out for the most abuse. He suffered from the lack of affection and nurturing of an uncaring mother during his formative years. Nash took seriously the duties of a parent to her children but his other siblings were not quite so sensitive to their mother's total lack of motherly instincts. Most of his siblings grew up with enduring the same lack of affection and nurturing and led dissolute lives. His older brother had the reputation of an accused murderer, drug dealer and all-around street thug. The older brother's lifestyle and reputation might be better understood if Gilbert Nash's recounting of one special incident involving his mother, brother and himself was true.

When Nash was a young boy of seven or eight, he was napping in the living room one day with his mother and older brother. Nash was sleepy but alert enough to witness an incident between his mother and brother. His mother was sleeping on a sofa on the opposite side of the room from his brother and himself when he saw his mother silently gesture to his brother to come over to her. Without speaking a word, the brother went over to his mother unzipped his trousers and took out his penis. She then performed oral sex upon her older son with her younger son watching. Nash's brother was about two years older and it seemed to him that this was not the first time his mother had engaged in such unspeakable behavior. Both laughed quietly and kissed when they had finished. Gilbert never forgot this incident which became the cornerstone of the trauma that was to consume the remainder of his young adult life.

With this as a backdrop to his childhood, Nash escaped his family by joining the Army. Unfortunately for him it was at the time of a great buildup of combat forces during the Vietnam War. He had joined the army as a patriot but quickly became disillusioned with war. The Pentagon was trying to maintain morale by inundating the troops and the country with meaningless euphemisms. Descriptions of the progress of the war such as "We've turned the corner" and "There is light at the end of the tunnel" were postscript to every evaluation of the Vietnam War by the Pentagon. History has revealed that the corner was never turned and the tunnel remained unlit until American forces finally abdicated the fight. Nash was having a very hard time dealing with the twin traumas of his childhood and people dying all around him in Vietnam.

While the military was declaring imminent victory, they were stunned by the Tet offensive in 1968 which saw the Viet Cong and North Vietnamese forces enter Saigon and other cities through an elaborate network of disguised tunnels which permitted the passage of equipment and personnel to reach the outskirts of Saigon without detection. The U.S. forces were caught completely off guard and suffered extensive causalities. Gilbert Nash and the American people began to question the invincibility of the United States military. Nash and his platoon fought valiantly trying to counter the gains made by the North Vietnamese and Viet Cong but one day found themselves pinned down by a company of Viet Cong during a fire fight.

Reinforcements were requested but none appeared. The Viet Cong eventually overran Nash's position resulting in the death of every member of the platoon except Nash. During the fire fight, Nash was struck in the helmet by a round of ammunition and knocked unconscious. At that time soldiers were issued large steel helmets with aluminum liners which were able to withstand the force of a rifle shot if it was fired from a distance. But the concussive shock usually sent you into dreamland.

Nash lapsed in and out of consciousness but he was lucid enough to realize that shots were still being fired and that he was at the bottom of a pile of his dead comrades. The Viet Cong were going around executing the bodies with rifle shots to the head making sure they were dead. Nash was still only semi-conscious but never moved awaiting his turn to be executed like his fallen comrades. Trying to think of a way to avoid sure death, Nash envisioned himself floating above the scene following a winged apparition he described as an angel. The winged figure seemed to be pointing a way out of his predicament but as his head began to clear, Nash's thoughts were of an earthier nature and trying to stay alive. The Kinnaree had disappeared but he knew the way out if he could somehow survive.

The Viet Cong shot everyone except Nash. He escaped death by lying perfectly still and trying to look as dead as his comrades. Inexplicably, the Viet

Cong never attempted to finish him off but they did take his rifle and ammunition and a few personal items and left him for dead. The Viet Cong stayed in the area for a few hours eating, drinking and surveying the spoils of war. As night fell they left leaving Nash without food, water or a way in which to defend himself. He laid there for what seemed to be an eternity, but he was alive. He went in the direction shown to him by the winged apparition and made it back to the American lines physically intact but emotionally broken. The army psychiatrists determined that he was no longer fit for military service and issued him a medical discharge. Nash returned to the United States, married and had children but his troubles were only just beginning.

Several years went by and the nightmares and night sweats became more pronounced as the time passed. Nash was a regular patient at the VA hospital but he also had a history with state and city hospitals. He held down odd jobs but with only a high school education, he could only get jobs befitting his educational status rather than his intellectual abilities. His deteriorating psychological condition was exacerbated by his single minded self-centered personality. This character trait probably kept him alive when he lay underneath his dead comrades but it also made him much more difficult to treat. One of the jobs he held upon his return to the U.S. was at the old Morgan post office on the far west side of Manhattan. Nash worked in the basement where huge bags of mail would be delivered. His job was to off load these huge bags onto platforms which created enormous amounts of dust. Every employee who worked in the basement suffered from a persistent cough or more serious sicknesses. Nash complained loudly to his supervisor who was unresponsive and they gradually grew to hate each other. Nash began to fantasize about killing his supervisor and he was told to quit that job by his mental health specialists but he was more interested in getting revenge on his supervisor than dealing with his mental problems.

One day, Nash could no longer control his irrational hate. He lay in ambush of his supervisor near the Post Office with the intention of killing him carrying a knife concealed in his pocket for that exact purpose. Nash waited but, unexpectedly, the supervisor had decided to take a sick day. Nash went to work that day as usual and the next when his supervisor appeared as usual. He never made another attempt to do in his supervisor although his testimony concerning the incident at trial seemed to indicate that he was making a great attempt to control his emotions. It wasn't a forgone conclusion that the supervisor would have met with an untimely death if he had not called in sick. But, given his diagnosis of PTSD, the odds were that someone in the wrong place at the wrong time would feel the cold steel of Nash's blade.

Nash had married and was raising two children after he had returned from Vietnam. Living with someone who was being treated for PTSD put a tremendous strain on the marriage. Trying to raise two children under those conditions made it virtually impossible. Nash's wife began to cheat on him disguising it in the form of finding fault where there was none. The arguments became more heated and violent until one day his wife left the home with the children to live with her boyfriend. He filed a petition with the Family Court for custody of the children. I didn't believe that Nash was entirely innocent given his ego and demanding personality but it was his wife who had left the home with the kids to live in an adulterous situation with a man that could only be considered a boyfriend and not a father to the children. The proceedings in the Family Court are closed to the public but are many times the scene of high drama as raw nerves frayed from broken promises are exposed. The flashbacks started as time ran out for Nash's wife. Nash stabbed her in the ante room leading to the courtroom of the Family Court causing her serious injuries.

Nash was convicted of assault and served several years in jail. Before he went to prison he entrusted his most valuable possessions which included alligator shoes, expensive sweaters and jewelry to the care of his mother. The items were placed in a trunk in one of the bedrooms of his mother's apartment. It can be said at this point that Nash was a real clothes horse with a taste for gold necklaces and rings. Where he got the money for these items from wages earned at entry level jobs was a matter of speculation but he always did fancy himself a ladies' man and dressed accordingly. His attitude was not changed by several years in a maximum-security prison. When he returned home from jail he discovered that his coveted alligator shoes, sweaters and jewelry had mysteriously disappeared from the trunk. He accused his mother and after several months of arguing, he struck his mother knocking her to the floor. His older brother, the one who had the shockingly degenerate sexual relationship with their mother, became enraged and began to menace him. The brother had a reputation as a violent drug dealer who was suspected of murdering a couple of his competitors but never prosecuted. One fateful night the two met in the bedroom occupied by the clothes trunk.

The brother confronted Nash about the physical violence inflicted upon their mother. Nash became very paranoid in response to his brother's threatening words and gestures. He knew what kind of person his brother was and when his brother reached into his jacket pocket the flashbacks started. Nash returned to the scene of his dead comrades protecting him from certain death during the war. His brother took on the form of a Viet Cong fighter. Nash took out his knife and plunged it into his brother's heart before his brother could make another move killing him instantly. Nash immediately left the apartment and ran down upper Fifth Avenue where he was very quickly apprehended by the police still carrying the murder weapon. When he was interrogated by the police, he made a full confession. From its inception you could say that this case was not a whodunnit, but a why. Nash told the police that he viewed his brother as an extreme threat which caused his PTSD to kick in and it was necessary to defend himself. He told the police about his psychiatric problems but they had absolutely no interest and instead used it as a convenient device to get Nash to open up even more so much so that when I began my representation of him, the case had been signed, sealed and delivered. It was the usual defense attorney's nightmare. More often than not, those charged with murder are coaxed by the police into making incriminating statements when they should be keeping their mouths shut and asking for an attorney. The police faked an interest in Nash's psychological problems. Nash assumed the police would be of some help which was the furthest thing from the truth.

When I took over the case, Nash had threatened his prior attorney as his symptoms grew steadily worse. Communications had broken down between them and I stepped into the breach. Nash was receiving some treatment for his condition but it was woefully inadequate. No one in the jail system had any sympathy for a murderer. I couldn't help but think that if the Department of Corrections knew the type of person Nash's brother was, he would have received the care that was required for a person with his very serious psychological problems. My first task was to go through the myriad of psychological records concerning Nash's long history. I soon discovered that he was being treated at a Veteran's Administration Hospital in Westchester County just north of New York City. The notes of his treating psychiatrist evinced a good deal of sympathy for Nash's condition beyond the usual reportage. I decided to call her to explore the depth of her willingness to help her patient or if I had misinterpreted the thrust of the detailed notes I had read in the records of his treatment. It is invariably very difficult to mount a defense of not responsible by reason of mental disease or defect and even more difficult to find a psychiatrist who is willing to provide the necessary testimony. In this case, all I had to do was make one phone call. Not only was the psychiatrist willing to help by providing such testimony, but she was willing to do it almost sight unseen. Of course, she was very familiar with Gilbert Nash but to agree to it in the context of a homicide trial on the basis of a phone call was extraordinary to say the least.

Shortly after that phone call, I filed a notice of the defense's intention to use the insanity defense. It was an affirmative defense but by this time, as a result of the Hinckley case, the defense had to prove their case. It was no longer the requirement of the District Attorney to prove sanity. Nash's treating psychiatrist, now turned expert witness, interviewed him about his mental status during the homicide which only reinforced her original assessment. Her report containing the reasons for her opinion was filed with the court and after several months of back and forth the case was ready for trial. The District Attorney started his case with the usual array of police witnesses. Nash's confession was deemed admissible in a prior hearing and since there were no other witnesses to the actual event much of their proof was furnished by Nash himself in the confession. Neighbors heard screams and Nash was seen running out of the building by several persons one of whom called the police. The confession itself was very comprehensive but it did not contain enough of the real substance of Nash's mental state at the time he killed his brother. In my opening statement to the jury, I told them that the defense intended to prove that Nash was legally insane and not responsible for his actions and we had the evidence to prove it via the testimony of our psychiatrist. I knew in my heart that it would be necessary for Nash to testify but I said nothing about that possibility. The case went to trial before the Hon. Joan Carey one of the finest jurists before whom I have ever appeared. It was always a pleasure to be in her courtroom. Justice Carey later went on to become one of the top administrative judges in the State of New York.

The real drama in the trial was the testimony of Nash himself. He spoke of the incident between his brother and his mother when he was a child. He told the jury that it had haunted him his entire life and had never come to terms with it. As a result, there was no familial affection between himself and the rest of the family. He was disgusted by his mother and he hated his brother. Then he told the story of his experiences in Vietnam. The jury sat enraptured by the story of his miraculous escape from death and apparition of the Kinnaree showing the way. Nash told the story with such intensity that you could see on the faces of the jurors that many of them were back in Vietnam with Nash reliving his fear. You could see the disgust on their faces when he told the story of the relationship between his brother and his mother. The fear he felt in the presence of his brother who he believed was a murderer and a threat to his own life. The part of his testimony which particularly resonated with the jury was the story of waiting in ambush of his supervisor at the Morgan Post Office who had unknowingly saved his own life by taking a sick day. That part of his testimony was told with great intensity as tears welled up in his eyes and his voice started to break when he told the jury about desperately trying to control his homicidal rage on that day but could not. All this he told the jury. His testimony was spellbinding. You could see that the jury had great sympathy for the trauma that was Nash's life. What he forgot to tell them was his belief that when his brother made the threats against him he returned to Viet Nam and thought that his brother was a Viet Cong soldier. I tried to get it into the record on re-direct examination after the District Attorney had finished his cross examination but Judge Carey ruled that it was beyond the scope of cross examination and my questions on that subject were not permitted. Judge Carey was right as she usually was.

I thought that I could get it into the record by asking our expert witness psychiatrist when she testified but as I delved into the subject of Nash's mental state I could see that she was having second thoughts about her diagnosis. Her testimony took on an air of uncertainty but she did testify that Nash was legally not responsible for his actions. When I asked whether there was a possibility that Nash had flashed back when he killed his brother, she said that she was not aware of any statement Nash had made to that effect nor could she say that there was a possibility that Nash could have had a flashback. At one point during her testimony Judge Carey had called a recess. Since our witness was still under oath, I could not speak to her about her testimony. I told this to her saying that she should try to relax as I had perceived that she was highly nervous. She screamed at me that it was impossible to relax. I was really taken aback by her attitude and proceeded to cut short my questioning and tried to get her off the stand before she had totally changed her opinion.

We had our insanity defense and Judge Carey charged the jury accordingly. There was plenty of read back testimony requested by the jury. In some jurisdictions like Washington, D.C., the rules do not allow for the jury to request to have their memories refreshed by having trial testimony read back to them while deliberating. New York always allowed read-back testimony and I could never understand why the District of Columbia would not allow it. If the juries would ask for read back in D.C., they were told that they should rely on their memories. If their memory was unclear, what sense would it make to rely on it? Strange rule. No need to waste time on thoughtful deliberations, I suppose. In New York, the jury could request that the whole trial be read back to them. During the deliberations in Gilbert Nash's case, nearly one whole day of deliberations was spent reading back testimony. You could tell by the nature of the jury's questions that they were leaning toward a verdict of Manslaughter, a lesser crime which was the final verdict. They had rejected the insanity defense but did believe that Nash had suffered from an extreme emotional disturbance when he plunged the knife into his brother's heart. It was the consensus of most who listened to the testimony including the court reporters, court officers and court clerk that if Nash had testified that he thought his brother was a Viet Cong soldier, the jury would have found him not guilty by reason of mental disease or defect. Their opinions are not to be taken lightly. They listen to more testimony than anyone else in the court system and their judgment is generally very accurate.

Judge Carey sentenced Nash to ten to twenty years in jail. In retrospect, the jury came to the right decision. Nash was not legally insane when he killed his useless brother. He truly did suffer from an extreme emotional disturbance brought on by his PTSD, but he probably knew what he was doing was wrong. If the jury had bought the insanity defense, he could have spent the rest of his life in a state psychiatric hospital waiting to be no longer considered a threat to society. Nash probably did society a service by dispatching his brother, but justice had been served by the verdict and sentence.

About fifteen years later I was sitting in a courtroom waiting for my case to be called when a middle-aged man sitting near me tapped me on the shoulder. He looked vaguely familiar and asked if I was a legal aid lawyer. I said that I was not but after a few seconds I realized that I was talking to Gilbert Nash. He really didn't recognize me and made no attempt to continue the conversation. Much can be said of the aging process but he never asked another question. He turned away and I never saw him again.

XI. DRIVING SOUTH IN THE NORTHBOUND LANE

It has most likely been every driver's experience that driving on the super high-ways of the United States can lead one to fantasize about how to relieve the boredom. I've often fantasized that on long drives the white lines in the middle of the road were actually lines of cocaine which the car was using to fuel its engine. After all you could plainly see the white lines disappear as the car passed over. A kindred spirit was a young man from New Jersey named William Garcia who went one up on me by acting out on one of my driving fantasies. Garcia didn't like cars getting in his way when driving on the high-way and his fantasy was to clear the road of all traffic. One warm summer night in 1984, he was in Manhattan with fellow New Jersey residents Felix Ro-driguez and David Laffman scoring cocaine in the usual places. They had grown weary after doing drugs all day in New York, so they decided to go back to their homes to sleep it off. Garcia, never the one to waste good drug money on public transportation, decided to hijack a yellow cab and proceed home in comfort. The trio, with Garcia in the lead, commandeered a cab at knifepoint. The cab driver strenuously objected to having his car stolen but Garcia quickly ended the conversation by stabbing him in the thigh and throwing him into the trunk. Garcia took control of the cab as any good leader would and headed directly towards the Lincoln Tunnel and I-95 into New Jersey.

The trio drove south on the highway at a rapid rate of speed with the cab driver still in the trunk. Since it was very early in the morning, traffic was rel-atively light given we are talking about New York City. As they continued south, unbeknownst to Garcia and his band of brigands, the cab driver had somehow managed to force open the hood of the trunk just enough to stick out his hand and wiggle his fingers. This was an era well before the invention of cell phones but citizen's band radios were very popular especially among truck drivers who would warn each other that "Smokey" was in the vicinity and they should slow down. Not all trucks had CB radios, but as fate would have it, there was one following directly behind Garcia and his friends. The truck driver got a clear view of the cab driver's fingers, thought this a very curious situation, and radioed the New Jersey State Police. The truck driver followed the cab from a distance and because of the hour not very many cars impeded his vision. But Garcia soon realized that he was being followed and headed for the interchange leading to the Garden State Parkway where large vehicles like the one following him were not permitted. The truck driver used his CB radio to keep the police up to date with the movement of the cab and they were on the scene within minutes.

During the chase, the truck driver was able to get a good look at Garcia, the driver, and Laffman who was sitting alone in the back seat but kept turning his head to view the action through the rear window. Rodriguez was in the front passenger seat but never turned his head. Several New Jersey State Police vehicles took up the chase with the cabdriver still wiggling his fingers. What a streak of bad luck for our heroes and those damned rundown yellow cabs with locks always in a state of disrepair. Garcia turned onto the Garden State Parkway heading south. The GSP runs the length of New Jersey further to the east of I-95 and much closer to the smaller communities in New Jersey. It is the main route to Atlantic City and the Jersey shore. No large vehicles such as the one that had been following Garcia and his gang were allowed on the parkway. There are local branch roads which run directly from the GSP to developed communities. Further to the south, you can get a nice view of the Pinelands, the home of the Jersey devil.

The mythical Devil in this case turned out to be all too human. Upon exiting I-95, Garcia attempted to elude the police by entering the northbound lanes while still driving south. The traffic was light because of the early hour and the police were able to close off the entire parkway after several near misses. Garcia was living my driving fantasy. He had eliminated all the cars around him and he had the Garden State Parkway all to himself. Living my fantasy through Garcia's criminal behavior didn't last long. Outmanned by police cars and overhead helicopters, the trio abandoned their purloined vehicle near one of the branch roads and headed for the backyards of the nearest homes leaving a trail of broken fences in their wake. With our trio now on foot, the police also abandoned their vehicles and called in the dogs, one of whom was named "Mike." Mike was a German Shepard with super-sniffer abilities. He caught the scent of Laffman and Rodriguez who had foolishly stayed together and were tracked hiding in separate tool sheds in the same backyard. It might have been a good hiding place under ordinary circumstances but with super dog Mike on the case, it was easy pickings for the police. Garcia managed to elude capture by staying on the move and somehow lifting his rather large girth over several more fences but Mike was a real hero. Lost in the melee was the cab driver who was temporarily left bleeding in the trunk but was soon enough extracted and taken to the hospital.

Laffman and Rodriguez were taken into custody. Laffman quickly gave up Garcia and his address. He was taken into custody a few days later at the home of one of his relatives near Jersey City. The trio was eventually extradited to Manhattan from New Jersey and I took up the representation of William Garcia. He proved to be a rather difficult client with all the character flaws of a drug addict with brains. Hostile and arrogant, he shouted unrealistic orders at me usually in the nature having his rights violated. He had a background as a community organizer so he was used to giving orders. His arrogance and bravado were of his own invention. When I told him something he did not want to hear like the vast amount of evidence against him, he would scream that I was working with the prosecutor and I was doing nothing for him. This is the usual pattern of drug addicted defendants who find it impossible to cope with reality. The only good news I could give him was that, indeed, as he had screamed at me many times, one of his basic rights had been violated when the New Jersey police failed to inform him of his right to an attorney when he was taken into custody there.

The case was sent to Justice Edwin Torres. Many of my most memorable trials took place in Judge Torres's courtroom. I doubt he specifically requested that any of my cases be directed to him, but the luck of the draw made it seem so. The proceedings started with pretrial hearings on the motion to suppress evidence. Garcia had made incriminating statements to the police when he was first taken into custody in New Jersey. The New Jersey police had failed to provide Garcia with an attorney when he was entitled to one. They also neglected to inform Garcia of his right to an attorney or could not produce evidence that they had. The Jersey cops were very slip-shod in dealing with the required protocol during the arrest procedure. Given their casual attitude, you could probably safely assume that they had no real interest in Garcia other than turning him over to the New York authorities as soon as they could. It was not difficult to have Garcia's statements suppressed because of the carelessness of the New Jersey police. You would think that given the chaos he caused on the Garden State Parkway they would want a good piece of Garcia but that was not the case. At the end of the testimony at the hearing, Torres turned to his courtroom attorney and muttered that he had to suppress the statements with a pained expression on his face. Torres had no choice or else you could bet your youngest offspring that he would have allowed it into evidence.

Rodriguez was represented by a very competent attorney named Tony Marano who had an office on Long Island. Laffman was represented by Robert Dilts who had formerly been the head of the office of the prosecutor of Bergen County in New Jersey. Dilts had been indicted and charged with corruption when he was in office. He was acquitted but forced to resign and was in private practice when he represented Laffman. He was a reformed alcoholic who exhibited all the characteristics of a practicing one. I did not learn of his reputation for deviousness and treachery until after the fact at the end of the trial. The trial went as expected. Judge Torres denied all defense motions while granting every request of the prosecution. The cab driver testified about his ordeal and how he managed to pry open the trunk because he knew that the lock was worn and would not close properly. The knife wound in his thigh caused a great deal of pain and bled profusely but had just missed a major artery for which he was grateful. He readily identified all three defendants and described their roles in his abduction and assault. Garcia wielded the knife while Rodriguez had helped subdue and throw him in the trunk. Laffman was sort of an onlooker taking no part in either the abduction or the assault. The cab driver told of fearing for his life when he was locked in the trunk. He believed that he would either bleed to death or die when the taxi crashed. Tony Marano and I could not understand why a white, upper-middle-class suburbanite would ever get involved with the likes of Rodriguez and Garcia. It was never fully explained but there was testimony that Laffman had used Rodriguez on prior occasions to score drugs in Manhattan. They were certainly not friends. When the cabdriver left the stand after testifying he glared at Garcia never taking his eyes off him until he left the well of the court.

At the conclusion of testimony, each attorney is permitted to make a closing argument called a summation. There is no strict rule as to which defense attorney should have the last word in front of the jury but it is generally agreed upon among them. Since I was first in my cross examination, I would be the last to give my summation. The theory being that since I was first to cross examine, the jury would not remember as much of my questioning so I would have the last chance to remind them of the points I had made, if any. This was one of those cases where there was so much evidence against my client, it probably would have been better to remain silent and be thought a fool rather than speak and remove all doubt. Laffman's lawyer, Robert Dilts, Esq. approached me and asked if he could go last. He postulated that there was far less evidence against his client and wanted to have the last word to the jury. It should be noted that upon the conclusion of all defense arguments, the District Attorney always has the last say because it is their burden to prove the case. We all agreed that Laffman had the best chance, so I relinquished the coveted last place in the pecking order to Dilts. I should have known that given the many flaws I had detected in Dilts's character during the trial, he had an ulterior motive. But I was still young and naïve.

Dilts proceeded to revile and repudiate Rodriguez and Garcia for leading his rich white client astray blaming them for all that occurred. Laffman seemed like the odd man out in this scenario but Dilts wanted the jury to know that he came from a higher economic class than "those other two Hispanics." The way in which he pronounced the word accentuating the "sp" and the "ics" left little doubt in the listener's mind that he thought Rodriguez and Garcia were just a couple of spics not on the same level as his client. In my summation, I could have easily called his client a common junkie and a rat for selling out Garcia almost with the first breath he took after being arrested, but I never mentioned Laffman's name. Neither did Tony Marano. When the offending word was uttered, I looked at Judge Torres, a Puerto Rican, but he never flinched. Dilts continued in this vein for the entire summation. Every few minutes, I jumped up to object to the most racist closing argument I have ever heard. My objections were overruled by Torres with a sarcastic grin. If a prosecutor had given a similar closing argument, the verdict would have been thrown out by an appeals court on the grounds of prosecutorial misconduct.

All three defendants were convicted of all charges as you might expect. Laffman had a fighting chance if Dilts had tried to separate him from Garcia and Rodriguez during testimony but he chose instead to use racism and bigotry to make his point. Laffman's family must have thought they had a real powerhouse in the former chief prosecutor of Bergen County, but he was truly a poor excuse for a defense attorney. Someone with reputation but little in the way of substance. Judge Torres sentenced each of them to lengthy terms of imprisonment but Rodriguez's conviction was reversed on appeal. The truck driver had identified Rodriguez at a show up procedure conducted by the police at the scene of the arrest. A show up is when the arrestee is identified by the victim while he is standing next to several police officers. The witness is brought to the scene and ask to view the defendant to confirm that the police have the right man. You'll remember that Rodriguez was sitting in the front passenger seat and was never seen to have turned his head. When the truck driver was brought to the scene he identified Rodriguez who was standing next to Laffman without ever having seen Rodriguez's face. So, although Rodriguez was identified by the cab driver when he got out of the hospital at a lineup a few days later, the show up in New Jersey was ruled to have violated Rodriguez's constitutional rights to such an extent that his conviction was set aside and a new trial ordered. Eventually Rodriguez avoided trial by pleading guilty to a lesser charge with a reduced sentence. With credit for the time he had already served, he got out of jail long before Laffman and Garcia had finished their terms.

Several months later I was discussing the case with another Assistant District Attorney. I mentioned Dilts's behavior during the trial and how he had suckered me. The assistant told me that Dilts had represented a man named Robert Ferrara who was convicted of murdering his gay lover. The facts leading up to the murder bordered on the bizarre. The victim was a transsexual named John Delia. Delia loved to cross dress and had sexual relations with both men and women. He began an affair with Ferrara who had a codefendant named Robyn Arnold. She was the daughter of a prominent physician and was a child of privilege. When Delia was having his affair with Ferrara, he began exploring the idea of a sex change. At that time, he unfortunately met Robyn Arnold. The two began dating, fell in love and got engaged. Delia again began to have doubts about his sexual identity. Arnold agreed that Delia should go through the operation and agreed to pay for it.

John Delia became Diane Delia and the following year married Robert Ferrara but continued seeing Robyn Arnold. Are you still with me? One warm autumn night in October 1981, Arnold and Ferrara drove Delia to a wooded area in upper Manhattan and each of them put two bullets into Delia's head. Don't ask me why. The jury convicted Ferrara and acquitted Arnold. He got twenty years to life. She married a wealthy dentist. The assistant with whom I was speaking told me that Dilts had convinced his co-counsel that he should go last and did the same thing he had done at my trial. Dilts argued that it was all Arnold's fault and reviled both her and her attorney. Finally, he told the jury that his client was not guilty because he had actually shot a dead body. Arnold's attorney had denied she was ever involved. No one in the courthouse was surprised by the verdict. Robert Dilts died in 2010 at age eighty-five. He was eulogized as a brilliant attorney. You make up your own mind. I have said my piece and will say no more.

XII. Tones For Jones Bones Or You're Never To Old For Love

As you get older and are fortunate enough to reach your seventies, you're supposed to slow down. The energy level wanes and thoughts of love turn more toward companionship than conquest. Most people in their seventies look forward to their golden years as a time for reflection upon their lives. Hot blood cools and life is lived with much less rancor. Eddie Jones of Harlem, New York City was a man in his seventies and looked very much like a man who would fit this stereotype. He had lived most of his life in New York City but the story of Jones's life read like a dime novel. He was a handsome man who was always impeccably dressed mainly to impress the ladies. He had been married couple of times and fathered a few children both in an out of holy wedlock. Jones fancied the life of a lothario and had many paramours throughout his life although he continued to live with his wife who spent most of her time confined to wheelchair and was totally disabled. This enabled him to live the life of a lothario by using his wife's disability payments to support his lifestyle. I don't want to completely mislead you. He did care for his wife but she was his only steady source of income. The attraction of women his age as he grew older did not interest Jones. He was always young at heart and preferred to spend his wife's money on much younger women who were more than happy to share in the bounty.

Jones was educated in the street but gave the impression of being a refined, educated person except if you crossed him or tried to replace him as a lover.

Then he would be more likely to put a bullet between your eyes. He also "never met a dame who didn't understand a punch in the mouth or a slug from a forty-five" to paraphrase a famous line from a Humphrey Bogart movie. He mostly treated his women badly but was always attentive to his disabled wife. Jones wasn't all bad but I cannot think of any other redeeming aspect of his personality. When he was seventy-two he got involved with a twenty something young woman from his neighborhood upon whom he lavishly spent his wife's money in return for sexual favors. These favors were usually bestowed at her apartment further downtown in Harlem. Eddie Jones had engaged in this kind of behavior for most of his adult life and several years before I represented him one of his former young girlfriends had tried to end their relationship because Jones had been messing around with other women while professing true love for her. They had many arguments about the other women and on one occasion he beat her to a bloody pulp. She got an order of protection for him to stay away from her and the love nest. He responded by getting a gun and breaking through the window of her fire escape and shooting her twice in the torso. She survived but Jones did several years in prison.

On the occasion of my entry into Eddie Jones's life as his attorney, he was going about business as usual with his most recent twenty something girlfriend when he discovered that he was not the only man in her life. You would think that any seventy-two-year-old man who was invited into the bed of a lady nearly fifty years his junior would be satisfaction enough but in his old brain, Jones was still a young stud and this was a matter of honor. Jones confronted his rival at a corner grocery store on West 135th Street in Manhattan and invited him to a duel but Jones was the only one with a pistol. He executed his rival just outside the store and escaped around the corner to his apartment on West 134th Street exactly one block away. The police were on the scene in a matter of seconds. There was no need to call 911 for the 32nd precinct was just down the block on W. 135th Street and a detective who was doing some paper work had heard the shots and came out running with weapon drawn. A master criminal was Eddie Jones. He shoots someone so close to the police station that a stray round could have smashed through one of the windows or lodged in the precinct door.

The ineptness did not stop there. It took the police over one month to track down Jones who appeared every day at his apartment to care for his wife.

Jones lived on the next street in the same block. You could say that it took the NYPD only one month to turn the corner on the investigation. Jones was arrested and was held in jail without bail. It was the usual jail-bail-no sale practice of the court for those charged with murder. One of Jones's shots had struck the victim in his face as a further indication of the irreconcilable affront to his honor. The incident had happened on the street just outside the store while the object of their affections was inside the store. She had heard the shots but did not see Jones fire the gun or slip away to his apartment around the corner. Jones was one of the very few homicide defendants I have represented that did not confess to the crime or make an incriminating statement to the police. But there was an eyewitness and the testimony of the girlfriend who was in the store not to mention the detective who had heard the shots and was on the scene almost before the smoke had cleared.

The trial took place before the Hon. Juanita Bing Newton who was a very knowledgeable jurist with a pleasant personality. This was one of two murder cases I tried in front of Judge Newton. I found her to be a fair jurist but she was no friend of the defendant when it came to sentencing. She ran a very tight ship with an eye towards efficiency and economy. My only complaint was that she generally refused to grant defense counsel's request for what is called "daily copy." Daily copy is the procedure whereby the District Attorney or defense counsel request that the prior day's testimony transcribed by the court reporter be made available the next day usually at the expense of the court. It is an expensive but necessary procedure especially in a murder trial. During my other murder trial before Judge Newton, there was a great deal of medical testimony about a subdural hematoma which is a blot clot on the brain caused by a blow to the head. The jury asked for several hours of read back of complicated medical testimony. If my request for daily copy had been granted, there would have been three pairs of eyes looking for it in the record instead of one beleaguered court reporter combing her notes for the testimony which took nearly the entire day to locate. The deliberations lasted three days and most of the time was spent waiting for the court reporter to go through her notes. It was an important issue because the jury in that case acquitted my client of the murder and convicted him of the lesser charge of manslaughter. What price justice?

The chief evidence against Eddie Jones consisted of an eyewitness who was sitting in a nearby parked car, the police and the star of the show, Jones's unfaithful girlfriend. The eyewitness was an upstanding young black man named Shane McDonald. He had met a young lady at work and decided to take her out on a date. The young lady asked McDonald to drive her to a hair dresser which was located on West 135th Street close enough to the shooting for him to get a good look at Jones as he was pulling the trigger. McDonald had parked his car and was waiting for his date to finish at the hair dresser's for more than two hours and got so frustrated that he was about to abandon her and her new hairdo when the shooting occurred. He later identified Jones from an array of police photos and later at a lineup. The detective who was doing his paperwork and came running when he heard the shots was the first to interview McDonald and Jones's girlfriend who had been inside the store. There was some urgency in scheduling Shane McDonald's testimony because he had been diagnosed with a grave illness and there was some real concern that at one point he would not be able to testify. Incidentally when I asked him during cross examination what had happened to his date, he said that he left with the police and never saw her again.

When Jones's paramour took the stand, I immediately realized that a star was about to be born. She was crude and obnoxious and her favorite words were "motherfucker" and "bullshit." A child of the ghetto, she was arrogant and hostile and had no love for the police, the office of the District Attorney or the courts. She consistently used words like "trickeration" when she thought I was trying to put words in her mouth during cross examination and "conversating" when she was having a conversation. She was attractive but not beautiful but from her appearance you could tell what had attracted Eddie Jones. She reluctantly testified that she had witnessed the original confrontation in the store and heard the shots a few minutes later. She also testified that she had a relationship with Jones for about a year and they would go to her apartment "to do, you know, the wild thing." She said she was aware that Jones liked to carry a gun and had seen it on many occasions. The jury was both repulsed and amused by her testimony but it did great damage to Jones's case. Then her performance soared to new heights when I got up to cross examine her.

As I was about to ask my first question, she turned her head away and muttered "here comes the bullshit" loud enough to be heard in the courtroom. Most of her answers to my questions were prefaced by "What the fuck you asking me that question for?" or "What the fuck did I just tell you?" When I questioned her about how she knew Eddie Jones carried a gun, she said "The motherfucker always carried a gun." I tried to achieve some degree of refinement in her testimony by repeating her answers but with a more objective flare.

"Did you ever see the motherfucker, as you put it, with a gun on this particular occasion?"

This achieved a modest amount of success because she stopped calling me an asshole under her breath after finishing her answers. The assistant prosecuting the case, Sandra Sneed, and I both agreed with Judge Newton that admonishing our star witness would only make things worse and she was permitted continue her performance unabated.

All hope for Eddie Jones living out his golden years as a free man was abandoned when Sandra Sneed got Judge Newton to admit into evidence the 911 call from Jones's attempted murder conviction. You could hear the terrified victim describe Jones entering her apartment through the fire escape window.

"He's pointing the gun at me," she screamed. "Please help. Oh my God. And then you heard the shots and the telephone receiver hitting the floor."

The jury did not waste much time in convicting Jones. I remember telling the jury that they could not believe the testimony of such a witness as Jones's girlfriend accentuating her hostility and abusive language. I really couldn't say much about Shane McDonald's testimony. At the time of his conviction, Eddie Jones was seventy-three years old. I argued for the minimum of fifteen years to life emphasizing that even the minimum sentence would probably be a death sentence. Judge Newton was a reflective jurist who took my argument seriously but she was hell bent on making an example of murderers and sentenced jones to the maximum of twenty-five years to life guaranteeing that his final days would be spent in jail. Defendants like Eddie Jones never learn from their mistakes and even if he had lived to be paroled at age ninety-seven, he would have never changed his behavior.

The Eddie Jones case was not the only case I tried with Sandra Sneed, the assistant prosecutor. She was a cut above the average and was always one step ahead of me when we were adversaries at trial.

Years after the Jones trial when I would meet her in the halls of justice, I would greet her by saying, "How you doing, wild thing?"

When she called on the telephone I would greet her with a "Here comes the bullshit."

She would laugh and tell me that no matter how many times I asked, she would not give me the address of where the girlfriend did "the wild thing." I would response by indicating that she took pleasure in ruining my life. Sandra left the office of the District Attorney many years ago. I am sure that she achieved greater glory than the prosecution of the likes of Eddie Jones who died in prison alone without love or honor.

XIII. Fields Of Ambrosia

Roger Fields spent much of his youth in Texas but moved to New York when he was a teenager after discovering that he was gay. Texas, in the 1960s, was not a place to be living an alternate life style. He was intelligent and gregarious and not at all shy about separating you from your money under false pretenses. What attracted people to him was his self-deprecating humor and his ability to make people laugh. It wasn't exactly a fatal attraction but those who had any experience with him would instinctively put their hands over their wallets when he entered the room. In Texas, he embezzled more than two million dollars from a sizeable church congregation by passing himself off as an ordained minister with promises of a new church. The congregation trusted a native son so they readily handed over their money relying upon his fabricated priestly credentials and his ability to raise Christ from the dead during his weekly sermons. He accomplished this while successfully concealing his homosexuality.

When I began my representation of him, he was on the run from authorities in Texas, Michigan, Florida and New Jersey where he had pulled off similar scams. Fields always managed to tightrope on the line between civil liability and outright criminal behavior. He used so many aliases that by the time the authorities uncovered his misdeeds, Roger Fields had dropped off the planet. He would always return to New York City where he could hide in plain sight and use his given name without suspicion. On the occasion of his return to New York, he made a stopover in New Jersey where he flashed his phony ministerial credentials and embezzled a small church congregation there. But New Jersey was merely chump change compared to the wealth he had envisioned for himself in New York. Using his startup money gained in New Jersey, he leased a Jaguar and made his grand entrance into the city that never sleeps augmented by his garrulous suits, cape and walking cane.

Fields got himself involved in Harlem politics and quickly rose to become a trusted community leader and a friend of Mayor Rudy Giuliani, Borough president Percy Sutton and community activist Evelyn King. He so impressed the community leaders and the mayor that he was given the responsibility of overseeing the construction of a group of smaller low-income houses in Harlem which were to be named after Evelyn King herself. Up to this point, Fields' grandest scheme was the swindling of the congregation in Texas where he convinced the parishioners to give and give some more while concealing his true motives and his lovers. In New York, that was no problem. He could be as outrageous and flamboyant as he wanted without raising suspicions. Even Giuliani himself was taken in and there was no real investigation into Fields's background done by the Office of the Mayor. It was hard to conceive that his behavior did not raise any red flags in the mind of such a law and order politician like Rudolph Giuliani who had been the head United States Attorney for the Southern District of New York but somehow it did not. Giuliani could smell a crooked deal from a considerable distance, but the connivance of Roger Fields gave off no such odor.

Fields coordinated the construction, paid off the Mafia and trade unions, appeased the community leaders of Harlem and somehow the houses were built. This was no small feat. The Mafia had their fingers in all the construction industries and the trade unions did not want any one working on the project that was not a union member. That eliminated most of the Afro-American workers promised to the community by Fields. Since Fields himself was an Afro-American, he could speak the language of the community but he also used city money to bribe union leaders to permit non-union Afro-American workers. When the contracts were awarded by the city everyone had a piece of the action including Fields who supplemented his large salary by skimming from contract payments adding to his war chest of ill-gotten gains.

Through his position as the administrator of the Evelyn King Houses, Fields gained control of all the financing involved. When the houses were completed there was a special ceremony which included Giuliani, Sutton, King and Fields. For many years, Evelyn King was a community activist with an excellent reputation. The Houses were named in her honor. Since Fields had control of the money, you can rest assured that he was not influenced by the praise heaped upon him by Giuliani, Sutton or King. He kept his eyes on the prize and when the Houses were completed he put his scheme into action quietly and without fanfare. He did this through the tenant application process.

Low income residents were required to submit their applications for tenancy though the New York City Housing Authority by a certain date. Then a lottery was to be held to choose from the thousands of applications. Those names not chosen would remain on the list and applicants would be notified as apartments became vacant. What was an opportunity for low income residents to improve their lives Roger Fields turned into a cash cow to support his lavish life style. He had control of the application process and prospective tenants carefully chosen from the thousands of applications were invited to Fields' office located in the King Houses. They were told that if they deposited "key money" with him, they would be given preference in the lottery and would be assured to be one of the lucky ones whose application would be accepted. This involved hundreds of prospective tenants who deposited varying sums ranging from several hundred to several thousands of dollars dependent upon the applicants means. Fields even gave the depositors receipts with his name affixed. Over the course of several months before the apartments were awarded, he managed to collect over three hundred thousand dollars of key money promising more apartments than had been built. Fields may have gotten his idea for the scheme from the movie *The Producers* when Max Bialystock (Zero Mostel) sold one hundred percent of his play to several investors which he thought was so outrageously bad that it would close on the first night. The play was a hit and Max ended up in jail with his partner Bloom (Gene Wilder) where they continued their scheme on a prison play produced by them swindling prison guards and even the warden who were all promised one hundred percent of the profits.

The movie was a laugh filled riot but Fields' actions were no laughing matter. Fields' scheme was a cash only business and it did not arouse any suspicions because most of the victims were desperately poor with no checking accounts or credit cards. Fields had scammed the poorest of the poor out of their meager savings and he got away with it for so long because he had informed his victims that the apartments were not yet completed or were still not up to code when all the time the apartments had been awarded in the lottery. But all such fast money schemes inevitably collapse.

Those who were deceived into believing that they were assured of an apartment began to complain when months had passed and they had not heard from Fields. He attempted to appease them by regretfully informing them the Housing Authority had insisted upon a lottery system and they were the losers but that their money would be refunded in due course. But due course was an eternity for the desperately poor who were expecting a better life and they complained to their community leaders, Mayor Giuliani, their Congressmen and anyone else who would listen. Fields was arrested and indicted for several counts of Grand Larceny and other related charges. One could hardly imagine a scheme like this working for more than a few months but Fields really didn't care. He spent lavishly but it was a time when those afflicted with AIDS had no hope and Roger Fields knew that he was dying.

From the very first moment I began my representation of Fields, I knew that he was going to be a major headache. He was held in jail on very high bail but not even jail or terminal AIDS could deter him. Somehow, he had convinced the New York City Department of Corrections that he was a sitting judge who had been unjustly accused and was allowed his own bathrobe, bedroom slippers, toiletry kit and private cell. Not bad for someone who was being deprived of his freedom in the snake pit that was and still is Rikers Island. He considered it beneath his station to appear in court when he was not in the mood citing his incurable disease when doctors had made it clear that he was perfectly able to make his regularly scheduled court appearances despite his illness. Many times, I tried to intercede with the Office of the Commissioner indicating that it was vitally necessary to his defense that he been present in court for his scheduled appearances. Fields countered by convincing his treating physicians at Rikers Island that he was in need of special attention when he came to court which was not available to him under ordinary circumstances. Finally, I told them that he was not a judge and that they were the victims of blatant manipulation. This was an unusual tactic for a defense attorney but I feared that Fields would miss so much of the preliminary proceedings that it would adversely effect his ability to cooperate in his own defense which is an absolute right.

Fields' grave physical condition was compounded by his hedonistic personality which spawned great melodrama. On several occasions, he would declare his suicidal intentions.

"Richard, I'm going to commit suicide. Do you hear? I am going to take my own life," he would announce with an air of resignation.

It was obvious to me that, although gravely ill and probably terminal, he was too much in love with himself to take his own life although he was refusing to take his AZT medication which was the only effective medicine available at that time for AIDS. The melodrama increased when he was transferred to Bellevue Hospital Prison Ward when his t-cell count had become dangerously low.

"Richard, I'm going to die in here," he gasped, holding his hand to his chest.

It nearly came to pass one day when he apparently annoyed a psychotic inmate who slashed him across his face with a piece of broken glass.

"Richard, look at what they've done to me. They're going to kill me in here," he predicted with all the melodrama and flare of a Shakespearean actor.

His words were prophetic but not before the criminal justice system had taken its pound of flesh.

While Fields was in Bellevue Hospital I engaged in plea negotiations with the Assistant District Attorney in charge of the prosecution. He told me that if Fields would surrender the money taken from the poor souls who were naïve enough to trust him, he could plead guilty to a lesser charge with a significantly reduced term of imprisonment. Countering the offer, I suggested that Fields' t-cell count was so low that he certainly would not survive the four-year term offered. Not only that but he was preferring to take his ultimate revenge on the criminal justice system by refusing to take his AZT medication. I conveyed my opinion to the assistant in an attempt to get a plea bargain which would include little or no jail time. I provided all of Fields' health records along with the poor prognosis from his doctor. But the Office of the District Attorney would have none of it. Constantly on the prowl for malingerers, they were of the opinion that Fields was not sincere in his threat to let himself die and would start taking his medication immediately after sentencing thereby possibly adding a few more months of life to what was an unquestionably fatal condition. They took the position that this would set a dangerous precedent.

The assistant countered by suggesting a term of imprisonment lower than originally offered but only if Fields revealed where the embezzled money was hidden. I knew that he would probably die before the newly offered term was completed but I was obligated to inform Fields and he surprisingly agreed to tell me where the money was located. One day I went to Bellevue Hospital to visit him three shopping bags in hand. I strongly suspected that the offer to reveal his secret was so much bullshit but I had an obligation to take him seriously although I was unwilling to admit to myself that I was playing the fool. Fields went through his usual routine of self-pity and spent most of the interview teasing me about the location of the money.

"Richard, I'm going to die a rich man," he postulated.

I reminded him that the money really didn't belong to him and then questioned why he was unable to bail himself out of jail if he had so much money? He responded by asking me to promise that if he told me the hiding place, I would use the money to, in fact, bail him out of jail. I responded that the District Attorney, upon discovering that he was out of jail and had more than likely used the stolen money to affect his release, would be on him like a rabid dog. But as his attorney, I did promise I would use it to post his bail although I was unclear as to its compliance with professional ethics. He seemed disappointed with my answer and never said another word about money, stolen or otherwise. It was at this point that I realized that he had gotten the bail idea from me and that the three shopping bags would forever remain empty of hidden treasure.

During a subsequent visit to Bellevue, Fields told me that the namesake of the Evelyn King Houses was, herself, a cocaine addict and that she had used his office on several occasions as a rendezvous point to meet her connection. In fact, he was so accommodating that he personally arranged the meetings himself. Fields knew everybody including the local drug dealers. He wanted to know if the District Attorney could use this information to get him a better plea deal? I have represented many of those who were charged with crimes who had used their knowledge of more serious crimes in order to strike a better deal for themselves. Since he was always asked to leave the room when the drug deal went down, he had no actual knowledge of the alleged drug transaction himself so his information was relatively useless. I went to the assistant prosecuting the case and obliquely suggested that Fields had knowledge of other crimes without mentioning names. He rejected the proposal when I told him that Fields was never present during the drug deals. It was very clear to me that their only interest was the return of the money. It was at this point that I told the assistant that there was probably no money left and very soon after a trial date was scheduled.

When the date was picked Fields seemed indifferent. As the date approached the indifference turned to deviousness. He knew exactly how to avoid court. He was still confined at Bellevue Hospital with its myriad of physicians with whom to unduly influence. He would invariably get one of them to report that he was too ill to come to court. One of the doctors thought that Fields could not withstand the stress of a jury trial. I knew that he was gravely ill but each time I saw him at Bellevue, he strutted in the hallways and barked out orders to his caregivers like a head of state. I didn't really care if he was deemed to be too ill to stand trial. Anything to avoid a trial and certain conviction, the creed of all defense attorneys especially when they have no defense. But the case was in the courtroom of the Hon. Richard Andrias who was a colleague from the Legal Aid Society before he was elevated to the bench. Whenever I was in front of Judge Andrias my first impulse was to say "Hi, Rick" instead of "your Honor." Judge Andrias ("Rick") was familiar with Fields' reputation and was having none of his peccadilloes. He engaged the services of a specialist who was a liaison between the court and the Department of Corrections to cut through all of Fields' maneuvering to assure his presence each day during the trial.

One day during trial Fields appeared in his specially issued bathrobe with "Bellevue Hospital" embroidered in large block letters on the back. His outfit was augmented by non-standard issue, faux fur slippers which adorned his feet complete with multi colored socks. Judge Andrias took one look and ordered the Department of Corrections, with the help of the liaison, to bring more appropriate clothing from Fields' locker at Bellevue. It would have been a real spectacle in front of the jury but they never got to see it. I thought that they had missed out on the only humorous moment during the entire trial. The trial, itself, was a procession of poor souls who had their dreams for a better life crushed by the wantonness of Roger Fields. The headaches continued, which included Fields whispering in my ear that he was going to die on that particular day. "Richard, I had a very bad night and I think that I'm going to die today." He would then look at me with the innocence of a child in the hope that I could stop the trial. After two or three days of whispering in my ear, without informing Judge Andrias, I imposed upon the liaison to have Fields evaluated upon his return to Bellevue after the day's session. The report was as I expected. There was no significant change in his condition and the sweet nothings whispered in my ear were written off as more Fields histrionics.

The most dramatic testimony in the trial was that of a young, single mother of three who had come from a broken home and had lived on public assistance most of her life. She lacked a high school diploma but was intelligent. After living in foster care for several years, she became pregnant in her early teens and from that point forward she was almost entirely dependent upon public assistance. She held down a few entry level jobs and managed to save almost one thousand dollars which she had earmarked for a security deposit on one of apartments at the Evelyn King Houses. She started to cry when told of giving Fields all her savings and the proceeds of her latest public assistance check. He gave her a signed receipt with a promise for a better life in the very near future. She choked up and could barely testify when she told of having to depend on Catholic Charities for food for herself and her children for more than six months after being duped by Fields. There wasn't a dry eye in the courtroom when she finished her testimony including many members of the jury. Fields never reacted to her testimony as befitting a true sociopath.

After one month of testimony, Fields was convicted on all counts. A few weeks later, Judge Andrias sentenced him to ten years in prison. It was one of the most difficult summations I've ever had to give. One could hardly question the credibility of such an array of sympathetic witnesses but I did remind the jury that some of the victims had violated the law by not reporting the money they had earned while collecting public assistance including the young mother whose testimony was the most dramatic. It was a feeble gesture and for one of the very few times in a lifetime of more than three hundred trials, I was almost too embarrassed to utter the words. Fields died of AIDS less than one year into his sentence. Criminals like Fields are imbued with such a belief in their own self-worth that, even in death, they believe that those that knew them would have sympathy for what might have been instead of what actually was. The only memory that would be left of Roger Fields life was the legacy of irreparable damage he had caused to so many of the least fortunate in society. His misguided sense of self-importance was the food of gods which fueled his engine. He wallowed in his field of ambrosia for a very short time and when he died, hardly anyone knew or cared except those whose lives he had ruined.

XIV. Mohamed Said: "Show Me The Money"

During my long career, I have worn out many briefcases of all sizes and shapes but it seemed that fate meant for me to be a shopping bag kind of lawyer. While I thought my presence would appear to be more dignified and business like with a briefcase, upon further reflection, shopping bags would have been more suitable notwithstanding the objections of the jurists before whom I appeared. Let's face it, shopping bags are better suited for carrying large quantities drugs, money and weapons than briefcases. Many of my clients would give their kingdoms for those ubiquitous sacks with which to further their nefarious endeavors, but never thought of bringing from home. Richard III would have given up his kingdom for a horse and in August 2008, this particular Richard would have given up his expensive briefcase for a shopping bag or two or maybe three or four.

At the time, I had been representing a resident alien from Yemen named Mohamed Musaid for about nine months. Musaid had been charged with murdering his wife's cousin a man named Rafik. Musaid had been working in New York City at various small grocery stores in Harlem since 1994 including the stores of his brothers which were located in the area of West 125th Street. The victim, Rafik, also worked in the same stores many times together with his cousin, Mohamed. It came to pass one day that Rafik and Mohamed got into a physical altercation in which Mohamed was the clear loser. Musaid had a wife and three young sons in Yemen whom he would visit about once per year. From all the information I could gather, Musaid was not very tightly wrapped and had emotional difficulties exacerbated by a lower intelligence when the murder occurred. It became plainly obvious that this was the case when I began my representation of him. No reason was ever given as to why the fight occurred, but there were rumors that Musaid was stealing money from his brothers and other employers and was ratted out by Rafik.

In retaliation, Musaid began to spread rumors that Rafik was paying to have his three sons sexually abused and sodomized in Yemen which is one of the great affronts in Islam. Anyone even accused of such behavior is considered an unworthy infidel. The sentence for anyone convicted in an Islamic court is death. In Japan during the age of the samurai, a vendetta could be declared and the offending party assassinated with impunity so long as the vendetta was first registered with the court of the Shogun. No trial necessary. Musaid should have lived in Japan during the age of the samurai. Over the course of the next several months, he worked himself up into such a state that he began to believe his own rumors. According to Musaid's brothers, the rumors were pure fantasy. The children in Yemen were safe but Musaid was having none of it. One day in November of 2007, Musaid purchased a gun in the street from a Hispanic man who was a self-employed gun dealer with no known address. The night before he ambushed Rafik, he called his mother in Yemen and told her that he was going to kill Rafik. His mother must have known the reason because the whole family was aware of her son's delusional thinking. Musaid always denied killing Rafik when I represented him and these were statements he made to the police when he was arrested. Musaid believed he was avenging Allah and it was his duty to rid the world of another infidel. Does this reasoning sound vaguely familiar in today's world?

But Musaid was not in Yemen before an Islamic court nor was he in Japan during the age of the samurai. Registering his vendetta with his mother did not exonerate him. He was indicted for Murder in the Second Degree and I took on his case in the early part of November 2007. Immediately after the shooting, Musaid took refuge in the vast subway system and rode the rails for more than twenty-four hours. When he returned to his rented room in Harlem the police were waiting for him. The police used an Egyptian officer to interpret for them. Musaid could understand and speak English but, in this circumstance, he preferred to use Arabic his native tongue. He told the police the details of the murder and his rationale for committing it. Most importantly, he told the police the location of the dumpster where he had thrown the gun as he was effecting his escape on the subways. The weapon was recovered and ballistic tests indicated that it was the murder weapon. Several years later, further testing revealed the presence of the Musaid's DNA on the trigger and handle. It was obvious to me that Musaid was suffering from a serious psychosis. He insisted upon his innocence and reasserted his accusations against Rafik but without indicating a basis for his beliefs. He could speak and understand English but, due to his mental state, he had difficulty communicating his thoughts. During my first interview with him, he vaguely spoke of "getting his money."

Musaid was mentally ill but, in my opinion, he had not yet reach the level of not understanding the nature of the charges against him or the functions of a defense attorney, prosecutor or judge. The solution to the problem was relatively simple. I knew that several weeks of incarceration without treatment in Rikers would drive Musaid completely crazy and before his second appearance in court, I determined that his condition was ripe for psychiatric evaluation. He was adjudicated unfit for trial and was ordered into the custody of the Commissioner of Mental Health for treatment for such a period until he was able to understand the nature of the proceedings against him. He was sent to the psychiatric hospital on Ward's Island in the East River near the Triboro Bridge with a great view of the Manhattan skyline. Musaid was housed in the prison wing called the Kirby Forensic Center where he had almost unfettered access to a telephone which afforded him the advantage of collect calls to Yemen to speak to his family. He also took advantage of making his one call per day to his lawyer which, of course, was me. Sometimes it was only twice per week. Other times I would not hear from him for weeks at a time.

The usual topic of conversation was not as you would expect. Musaid had no idea about the criminal justice system having grown up in a completely different culture. I made no attempt to explain it to him because he had no idea of the basic concept of a jury trial, the Bill of Rights or the Constitution for that matter. His ignorance of the system would mean that it would be that much more difficult to teach him the basics notwithstanding his very serious mental illness which was exactly what I wanted. More time in a hospital rather than prison would provide a more humane environment not to mention the fact that I wanted as much delay as possible. Every time Musaid called the topic of conversation would be "his money." He would tell me about the existence of approximately fifty thousand dollars he had in a bank. "I want my money," he would constantly repeat during our conversations. This only reinforced my belief that Musaid was psychotic and I paid little attention to his delusional ramblings. The phone calls became a nightmare of constant repetitions of "I want my money, I want my money." It was truly annoying but I was overjoyed at the fact that his treatment was having no effect which would keep him in the hospital for an indefinite period of time.

One day in the summer of 2008, I received my usual call from Musaid and I was so sick of listening to "I want my money" that I decided to humor him by asking specific questions about the location of the money. I was expecting befuddlement but what I got were very specific answers to my questions with no hint of delusion. I said to myself, "This guy is serious. He really has something to say." Musaid went on to tell me of the location of the Chase bank on West 125th Street and the number of the safe deposit box where the money was located. Incredulously, I called my crack investigator, Mike Barry, and sheepishly told him to check out the bank to verify the existence of the safe deposit box. Mike is a real romantic and loves movie scripts, so I knew he would be on it in the blink of an eye. Mike confirmed the existence of a box under the name of Mohamed Musaid. The plot was thickening. When Musaid called the next time, I asked him about the location of the keys to the box. He told me that the police had taken them from him when he was arrested. My excitement turned to disillusion as it seemed obvious that the police had taken possession of whatever was in the box months before. I envisioned a detective's wife driving around in a new SUV paid for with cash. But why did the bank still have a record of the box under Musaid's name only?

One very hot August day in 2008, Mike Barry picked me up at my apartment to interview Musaid. The bank had told me that I would need a durable power of attorney with M. Musaid's notarized signature properly witnessed in order to gain access to the safe deposit box. I had brought several with me from my office. Enter the shopping bags. In order to make an impression on the bank officers, I wore my favorite Armani knock-off suit which I had purchased from a budding clothier with no fixed address on Canal Street at a severe discount a few weeks earlier. The clothier was so happy to do business with me that he gave me a few Armani knock off shopping bags at no extra charge. I told Mike to get dressed up also. We drove to the Kirby Forensic

Center on Ward's Island to get Musaid's notarized signature on one of the durable power of attorney forms located in my briefcase. Also located in the briefcase were the fake Armani shopping bags which I had somehow squeezed into the bag to avoid the embarrassment of having to explain why they were there. As Musaid was reluctantly signing the form, I tried to explain its meaning and the meaning of a durable power of attorney. He understood none of it but he did know that if he signed it, he was going to get his money. Mike notarized the document and we were off to the bank on our treasure hunt.

We parked the car as close to the bank as legally possible but it was still almost a ten-minute walk away. We were both a little apprehensive about the distance we would have to travel if the phony Armani bags were filled with real money. My anxiety was tempered with the knowledge that Musaid was as crazy as a bedbug and I was probably on another fool's errand. We entered the bank looking very official. Surprisingly, we learned from the manager there was no record in the logs of any police attempt to open Musaid's box. Had the police really screwed up that badly? I told the manager that I was Mr. Musaid's personal business representative as evidenced by the notarized power of attorney. I made a silly joke about being a power attorney with the power of an attorney and we were quickly on our way to the lower floor of the bank where the safe deposit boxes were located. During my conversation with the bank manager, I somehow neglected to mention that my client and business associate was in a psychiatric hospital charged with murder. How could I be so forgetful? But I did not forget to tell him that Mr. Musaid had lost his keys to the box on his last visit to Yemen and had fallen ill and had elected to call his lawyer to retrieve the contents. The manager acted very professionally and did not ask questions after he saw the power of attorney. The manager had prearranged for a locksmith to break into the box. That took about another thirty minutes the cost of which was charged to my credit card and we were escorted to a very small room to be left in private with the contents of the box yet unopened.

The room contained a small table with one non-matching chair. There was barely enough room for the two of us to fit with our brief cases and shopping bags. Mike was a bit on the heavy side at that time so it was impossible to turn one hundred eighty degrees without bumping into each other. Speaking of degrees, the outdoor temperature was about ninety degrees and while the bank was air conditioned, the room was unventilated. Our situation put me in mind of a scene from another opera, Verdi's Aida when Radames, the hero of Egypt, was punished for being a traitor to his country by falling in love with the slave temptress Aida, usually sung by a three-hundred-pound soprano, the daughter of the treasonous Amonasro. Their fate was sealed forever when they were left to die in an airless tomb. While Mike was not in the same weight class as the slave temptress, the room was too small for just one person and was as airless as the lovers' tomb.

With great anticipation, we placed the box on the table and lifted the cover. What happened overwhelmed all expectations. Tightly bound one hundred bills came at us like projectiles from an automatic pistol. The one-hundred-dollar bills along with wads of fifty and twenty-dollar bills were so tightly packed into the small area of the safe deposit box that the accumulated pressure created its own energy when it was released. There was so much money in the box that the bills fell onto the table and the floor from their own momentum. Mike and I stood there in stunned silence for at least thirty seconds. Then we faced each other with looks of complete disbelief at what we had just witnessed. We gathered ourselves and tried separating the money into equal stacks so that we could attempt an accurate count. I thought, "What the hell was I going to do with all this money?" Musaid had sworn that he was without funds for an attorney so my services were paid for by the city. Since I was representing a supposed indigent defendant, I would most certainly lose my license to practice if I took it in lieu of payment from the city. If I claimed both, I would undoubtedly be indicted for grand larceny. Who would think that an uneducated psychotic like Mohamed Musaid who lived like a pauper, could have accumulated so much wealth on his own? All his protestations amid his delusional thinking were true which was all the more incredible.

An accurate count was virtually impossible given the conditions. There was no room for the money on the small table. We could not distinguish between the counted and uncounted stacks because there was no space to separate them. Musaid had personal items like his Yemen passport, green card, visa applications for his kids and VHS tapes of his children in Yemen mixed in with the money. Wads of uncounted bills remained on the floor or what we thought were uncounted bills. We weren't quite sure. Finally, after two hours of sweating through our clothes growing feint from the lack of oxygen, we decided on our last resort. I pulled out the shopping bags and dumped all the money into them. Our plan was to have Mike go to the car and stop in front of the bank whilst I stayed inside with the money. When we emerged from our room like tomb, or tomb-like room, take your choice, we were able to breathe normally and quickly realized that all we had to do was bring the money upstairs to the bank counter to get an exact figure. I guess it must have been the temporary lack of oxygen which caused our dimwittedness. The final figure was not fifty thousand but it was forty-eight thousand, seven hundred dollars which included approximately fifteen hundred dollars in Musaid's checking account. Now, what to do with the money.

As my brain cells began to absorb more oxygen, the synapses started firing on all cylinders and I thought of my ancient escrow account lying dormant for many years with, as luck would have it, the Chase bank. I filled out a deposit form and left the money in the same bank where it had resided for who knows how many years. I left the bank with my receipt but not before I asked for the return of my fake Armani shopping bags. Mike and I were very happy that we did not have to negotiate the streets with so much money, especially after we had made its existence known to bank employees particularly those who put it through the automatic counter. The Armani camouflage would have been useless once the word had gotten out. I then thought of the fate of Radames and Aida and vowed to never to get myself into a situation like that again. Thus, began a seven-year odyssey with the fate of the money as the centerpiece of my relationship with Mohamed Musaid. Although always confined, he still wanted his money.

After retrieving the money, I went back to Kirby Hospital to tell him where it was located. He became immediately distrustful and paranoid. He insisted that the money be delivered to him at the hospital. He complained to his treating psychiatrist that I was somehow depriving him of his money. Shortly after my visit I received a phone call from the psychiatrist and in an accusatory tone, he asked what I had done with the money. Then he asked if I was assigned counsel the inference being that I had used my status as his court appointed attorney to gain access to his money. I was really put off by his attitude but I did ask for his fax number so I could send a copy of the deposit ticket which I advised he should put in Musaid's file. I then reminded him that he was one of the witnesses to his patient's signature on the power of attorney and if I had any ulterior motive, I would certainly not have left such an obvious paper trial. I didn't really care if he believed me but it was a harbinger of things to come.

I really didn't know what to do with the money or if it was even ethical for me to have it without informing the Assigned Counsel Plan who had originally assigned me to the case. If I had told them, I would probably be forced to turn it over to the state or the city to help defray the high costs of maintaining Musaid in the psychiatric hospital. But I thought of his wife and children in Yemen. I frankly told Musaid that he stood a very good chance of spending the next twenty years or so in a New York State prison and that it would be a good idea for him to send the money to his family. He still did not understand that it was not possible to keep the money with him in jail which he had insisted upon. I proposed to send the money in small increments to his family but Yemen had no viable banking system and there was the problem of the growing influence of al-Qaeda and the threat to his family if they suspected a large amount of money was being transferred. He was not forthcoming with answers to my inquiries and while he never answered in the negative, his vagueness indicated to me that he wanted to continue to exercise some control over his money and wanted to keep its existence secret even from family members. Musaid's brothers seemed to have no knowledge of the money when I interviewed them and I never told them. They did tell me that Rafik's family had engaged the services of a New York attorney to search for any assets Musaid may have hidden but I never heard anything more about it.

Over the course of the next eighteen months, Musaid drifted in and out of competency. When he was determined to be competent and sent back to Rikers, I would merely wait for him to stop taking his medication which would inevitably happen and he would again become delusional and paranoid. I would then request the judge to order another competency evaluation and Musaid would be sent back to the Kirby Forensic Center. During his periods of competency, I would always ask him if it was agreeable for me to send the money to his family. One time he did agreed, but when I asked about the mechanics of how to transfer the money, he would look at me with a pained expression and say that it would cost too much money. I asked him how he did it before he was arrested but he would never answer the question. He nearly became hysterical when I suggested that the money be given to his brothers who could take it back to Yemen. The secret of the money remained locked in my escrow account collecting dust. He never appreciated the fact that if the police had opened his safe deposit box before I got to it, there would probably be no money left to worry about.

Another year passed before Musaid was returned to court from the hospital. Musaid went back to Rikers and predictably stopped taking his medication. I, just as predictably, requested another competency evaluation. The revolving door between the court and the psychiatric hospital was still in fine working order but this time when Musaid stopped taking his medication, his paranoia and delusions became more profound. When I spoke to him he seemed to have great difficulty understanding the words. The Arabic interpreter told me that his answers made no sense. His cognitive abilities had become severely impaired in both languages. He made his appearance in court dressed in his hospital gown, slippers and bathrobe. He walked very slowly to his seat in the courtroom and looked dazed when he faced the judge. As I was making my umpteenth request for another competency evaluation, Musaid fell out of his chair onto the floor. I didn't have to say another word. The judge ordered another evaluation. This time I was present at the psyche clinic in the court manned by the department of Corrections when the psychiatrists examined him. For the first time, Musaid never mentioned his money. His response to most of the psychiatrists' questions was "My head turns around." He had no cognitive understanding of his situation or even the charge of murder against him. He again was determined to be unfit to stand trial but this time the prognosis was very poor. He was sent to the mid-Hudson psychiatric hospital for intensive treatment where he stayed for the next two years. He would call me every few months and through the stupor brought on by the powerful medications given to him he would ask about his money. The existence of the money seemed to be the only island of sanity in an ocean of insanity. It would set the stage for the next phase of his odyssey through the criminal justice system.

It was now 2012 and Musaid had been in custody for nearly five years. He began to exhibit psychosomatic symptoms when he was sent back to court from Mid-Hudson.

"I am a sick man," he would say. "My kidneys hurt," he would tell me during one phone call.

He would complain that he had a bad heart always reiterating that he was a sick man. These complaints were as dominant a theme as the demands for his money. The money demands became much more aggressive. The phone calls evolved into sheer harassment and it was necessary for me to suspend his telephone privileges because of their frequency. In the beginning, Musaid would be allowed to call Yemen to speak to his children but those calls had ended long ago so my number was the only one called. At one point, early on before he became completely psychotic he would call the Consulate of Yemen and complain about his money. He harassed the young lady who answered the phone so much that she would call me to see if I could get him to stop. She told me that it was useless to send the money to Yemen by ordinary means. The only method with which she was familiar was physically transporting cash to Yemen. If that was the method used by Musaid, it seemed that he had not used it for many years. I told the judge that Musaid was still incompetent because of his psychosomatic delusions which I was told by one of his treating doctors was incurable. For one final time, Musaid was sent back to Mid-Hudson. Between you and me and Musaid's medication, he was in much better condition than I had ever seen him but I wanted him to stay in the more humane environment of the hospital rather than prison. The treating psychiatrists were in sympathy with me as their diagnosis reflected.

Finally, in December 2014, at the start of Musaid's eighth year in custody, the judge was tired of the revolving door and he called for a competency hearing of his own accord. He disagreed with the psychiatrists and declared him fit for trial. Musaid would always declare the "he wanted to go to the trial" with no understanding of the procedure. All this time the case had been in front of the same judge, The Hon. Gregory Carro, and he was about to fulfill Musaid's wish. By this time, Musaid hated me for "stealing his money." I don't think anyone believed that he had any money but he did tell the judge that I had stolen it. He asked Judge Carro for a new attorney and his request was granted. Just before I was taken off the case, I knew that I had to do something with the money. I wanted to give it to his brothers but was unable to contact them. Shortly afterward, Musaid told me that they had moved to Saudi Arabia. The new attorney took over the case and one day he appeared in my office with a friend of Musaid who had a more recent power of attorney signed by Musaid and I wrote him a check for forty-eight thousand, seven hundred dollars. The friend was another man from Yemen who indicated that Musaid had been demanding his money from him even before he took possession of it.

Mohamed Musaid was convicted of Murder in the Second Degree in February of 2016. Judge Carro sentenced him to the maximum of twenty-five years to life and another four years for possession of the weapon. Evidently Musaid acted up in court by falling on the floor complaining of the imagined pain in his kidneys and heart. In my opinion, he was incurably psychotic but like most of the other defendants, I have represented with a mental illness, Musaid would not agree with, or cooperate in, his defense. The severely mentally ill have little insight into their psychosis and refuse to come to terms with their illness. This inevitably results in a very bad ending, as it did for Musaid. I will never forget that hot August day in 2008 when I opened the safe deposit box. You truly would have to have been there to believe it. I am sure that the money was the source of the hatred between Musaid and Rafik. We will never know. Musaid sold his soul for the money and in return he lost his family, his freedom and ultimately his life. If he survives his prison term, he will be deported to his native land where Rafik's family will be waiting.